The Challenge of the Cults

The Challenge of the Cults

MAURICE C. BURRELL

BAKER BOOK HOUSE
Grand Rapids, Michigan 49506

Paperback edition issued 1982 by
Baker Book House Company
with permission of copyright owner

ISBN: 0-8010-0816-6

Printed in the United States of America

Quotations from the Bible are from the New English Bible, © the
Delegates of the Oxford University Press and the Syndics of the
Cambridge University Press, 1961, 1970, unless otherwise stated.

Contents

63861

Preface

A few years ago, my good friend and former theological-college principal, Canon J. Stafford Wright, invited me to collaborate with him in writing *Some Modern Faiths*. That book was given a kind reception in Britain and overseas and still seems to be meeting a need. It deals with what the Oxford sociologist, Dr Bryan Wilson, calls 'established' sects, such as Jehovah's Witnesses, Christadelphians, Mormons and Christian Scientists. Though these sects originated in the USA in the nineteenth century, they are still very much part of the religious scene here and in other parts of the world.

Recent years have seen a fresh crop of sects, including the seven examined in this book. Although some of them (the Family of Love, the Armstrong movement and Scientology) were started in the United States, others (Transcendental Meditation, the Divine Light Mission, the Hare Krishna movement and the Unification Church), though now strong in America, originated in India or farther East. As we should expect, therefore, some of them are 'Christian' sects in the sense that, although they have rejected much of what mainstream Christianity stands for, it is from the Christian religion (rather than any other) that they have parted. Because of this, they still use much of the terminology of Christianity, though they often mean something different by it. Others have more in common with other world religions, in particular with Hinduism, and look for leadership to a guru-like figure.

There is widespread ignorance about the beliefs and

practices of these sects. They are often confused with each other and sometimes people fail to distinguish them from mainstream Christianity. There is need for clarification. This book, therefore, seeks to do with these seven more recent sects what *Some Modern Faiths* did with their nineteenth-century predecessors. I have endeavoured to describe clearly how each originated, what their adherents believe and practise, how they seek to spread their views, and in what respect they differ from orthodox Christians. Before looking at each one individually, however, we begin with a chapter outlining what these seven sects have in common. I have also tried to end on a positive note by indicating some of the ways in which they challenge mainstream Christians to look hard at their own beliefs and practices.

Inevitably, I have made it clear that there are very important differences between the sects I have examined and my own faith, which is that of a Christian. That has been necessary (as well as inevitable) because I am concerned about truth and because, as a Christian, I believe that truth is to be found pre-eminently in Jesus Christ. This does not mean that I question the basic sincerity of members of these sects. I have learnt to respect those who have been willing to discuss their views with me, even though I have had to part company with them on many vital issues. Sincerity, however, is not enough, for it is possible to be sincere yet wrong. I believe that in many ways they are wrong, and in the following pages I have tried to explain why. My evaluation has used as its yardstick the Christianity of the Bible and the historic creeds, because I believe that in them the truth is enshrined. I have tried to be honest and fair, however, and if unwittingly I have misrepresented the views of any of the sects examined I am truly sorry.

Maurice Burrell

1 Some general characteristics

Sects have been described as movements of religious protest.[1] Although the particular form of the protest may vary from sect to sect, it is always marked by a rejection of the authority of mainstream religious leaders and sometimes of the secular government as well.[2] That is as true of the seven sects examined in this book as it is of any of the others found within western society today. Moreover, sects not only separate themselves from the mainstream of religion and society, but also from each other, even though sects often have much in common. Each has its own particular emphases in faith and conduct, and each makes exclusive claims. Because they are all protesting against the common enemy, which they believe to be conventional religion, materialistic society, or (quite often) a combination of the two, however, they all exhibit certain general characteristics. It will be helpful to consider some of these common features before looking more specifically at each sect in turn.

Missionary zeal

Perhaps the most obvious characteristic of the sects is the zeal with which their members pursue their proselytizing activities. Believing that they alone have the truth of God, the one message which the world needs to hear and without which it is doomed, members of the sects with which this

---

[1] Bryan Wilson, *Religious Sects* (Weidenfeld & Nicolson, 1970), p. 7.
[2] *Ibid.*

9

book is concerned give themselves unstintingly in missionary activity. This is especially true of the Family of Love (the former Children of God), the Divine Light Mission, the Unification Church and the Hare Krishna movement. Their members spend many hours daily in street work, selling their literature, spreading their message and seeking to win recruits. Often their methods are dramatic, as with the doom vigils of the Family of Love and the continuous chanting of the Hare Krishna movement. Although, in comparison, the methods of Transcendental Meditation, the Armstrong movement and Scientology are much less obvious, their aims are identical. Each sect takes very seriously the business of spreading its message and making disciples.

Although it does not furnish Christians with any kind of excuse for their own lukewarmness and lack of missionary zeal, it is nevertheless fair to ask what motivates sect members in their proselytizing activities. They would all claim that the motivation springs from the belief that they possess God's truth for modern man and have been chosen by God to reveal it to the world. As we shall see as we look at each of the sects in detail, however, all have rejected the Christian gospel of God's grace and justification by faith alone and have put in its place the old heresy of salvation by human effort. Inevitably, therefore, there is an element of self-interest in their witnessing, for when a sect member sells his literature, speaks of his faith, or (especially) makes a convert, he believes that he is in some sense contributing to his own salvation as well as that of his contact.

It needs to be emphasized, however, that mixed though their motives may be, most sect members display commendable zeal in their attempts at outreach, the kind of zeal which is often singularly lacking among mainstream Christians. To most neutral observers, we who belong to the mainstream Christian churches generally appear to lack both the sincerity and the vitality of sect members. Nor do they hear us speaking with the same kind of assurance about our faith as that which they detect when they listen to sect members. A well-known commentator on sect activities makes the point: 'Sectarians put their faith first: they order their lives in accordance with it. The orthodox, in contrast, compromise faith with other interests, and their religion accommodates the demands of the secular culture.'[3]

Charismatic leadership

The second important characteristic these sects have in common is the importance attached to the leader. The eminent sociologist, Max Weber, first drew attention to this trait in reflecting upon sects generally. He said that the founder of a sect achieved a position of authority over his followers which could best be described as 'charismatic', for the leader was believed by his followers to be set apart from ordinary mortals and to be endowed with super-natural, superhuman, or at least very exceptional powers or qualities.[4] Weber said that the charismatic leader was then able to win obedience from his disciples on the grounds of his 'divinely inspired mission, his heroic deeds, his extra-ordinary endowments.'[5]

Because of the loose way in which the term 'charismatic' is used today, Weber's terminology has to be handled with care. Nevertheless, used as Weber meant it to be used, it can hardly be bettered as an accurate description of the place occupied in these seven sects by their respective leaders. The Divine Light Mission claims that its leader is a twentieth-century incarnation of ultimate reality; the Unification Church, that its leader is the Lord of the Second Advent. The Hare Krishna movement calls its leader 'His Divine Grace' and suggests that he too may be an incarnation of the divine, an avatar in the Hindu tradition. During their 'Children of God' period, the Family of Love regarded David Berg as the prophet Moses David, through whose Mo-letters God spoke and through whom, therefore, extensions of Scripture were mediated. Claims by the other sects in this book seem to be more guarded, but it will be

[3] *Ibid.*
[4] Max Weber, *The Theory of Social and Economic Organisation* (Collier Macmillan, 1964), p. 358.
[5] Dennis Wrong, *Max Weber* (Prentice Hall, New Jersey, 1970), p. 43.

shown in subsequent chapters that Armstrong's views are regarded by his followers as the only legitimate interpretations of Scripture given by God to correct nearly two thousand years of apostasy within the church, that Hubbard's teaching is regarded by Scientologists as the complete fulfilment of all that religious leaders through the centuries have eagerly sought but failed to find, and the Maharishi offers to Transcendental Meditationists the way that can set people free. It will also become apparent as this book proceeds that sect members are not just adherents, but dedicated disciples and devotees of their leader.

In contrast to this strong, charismatic leadership characterizing sects, the complaint often levelled against mainstream Christianity today is that it lacks leadership in this dynamic sense and has allowed itself to become over-institutionalized. This should not surprise anyone who has read a little of either church history or sociology. Highlighting the role of the charismatic leader, sociologists have shown that, with the passage of time, the charisma has become routinized or institutionalized, and in this respect the Christian church is no exception. What is often overlooked is the fact that this is also a fairly well-established pattern in the history of sects. Elsewhere[6] I have pointed out that the more established sects such as Jehovah's Witnesses and Mormons provide clear examples of the movement away from charisma to bureaucracy. After the death of the founders of these two sects, their successors set about the task of strengthening the institutional side of their respective sect's life, until in time the personal relationship between leader and led gave way to an elaborate structure with barriers between top officials and rank-and-file members. The beginnings of that kind of development can be detected already in some of the sects examined in this book. Only time will tell whether, when their present leaders die or are replaced, these more modern sects will continue along the path of institutionalization towards a thoroughgoing bureaucracy and thus become 'established' sects, or whether

---

[6] Maurice Burrell, unpublished PhD thesis, *Authority in Two Religious Sects* (University of Lancaster, 1977).

(like many sects before them) they demonstrate the transitoriness of much sect life and cease to exist altogether.

Applying the same kind of sociological insights to the history of the church, it is not difficult to see that, with the passing from the earthly scene of its Founder, a similar movement from charismatic leadership towards bureaucracy was almost inevitable. Indeed, many Christians would wish to point out that for them the only person with charismatic authority, in that strictly Weberian sense, is their Lord and Saviour, Jesus Christ. One of their chief complaints about the sects is that they allow fallible human beings to occupy that place of leadership which rightly belongs only to Christ. Their own history has taught Christians how dangerous it is to regard any human being as the sole arbiter of truth, the infallible interpreter of Scripture, or the one spokesman for God. Whilst recognizing, therefore, that there is some truth in the allegation that today's church lacks leadership, in the sense that there is no one human leader to whom all Christians look, Christians will wish to point to their own discovery (perhaps rediscovery) of shared leadership under the over-all lordship of Christ. With Paul they wish to acknowledge that Christ alone, as 'the image of the invisible God', is 'the head of the body, the church'.[7]

Exclusive truth

It is easy to see how belief in a charismatic leader with a unique message has led each of the sects to develop the view that it has an almost exclusive claim to truth. It is necessary to qualify 'exclusive' with 'almost' because, although I believe it will be shown in subsequent chapters that this exclusiveness is found in all sects, it is more obvious in some than others.

According to the Divine Light Mission, the true 'knowledge' of God can be imparted only by Guru Maharaj Ji himself or by others commissioned by him to do so. The Family of Love believe that they are the true Jesus People,

[7] Colossians 1:15, 18.

13

for whereas all other allegedly Christian groups have distorted the truth of the Bible, they alone take their Christianity seriously. Armstrong believes that God has chosen him to recall an apostate Christendom to repentance, faith and obedience, and as far as he is concerned this can be done only by joining the sect. Members of the Unification Church believe that Sun Myung Moon is the Lord of the Second Advent, the twentieth-century Messiah, who has come to bring the full salvation which Jesus failed to achieve. In the case of these four sects, the claims are unequivocal and the challenge is clear: the real needs of humanity (however each sect sees these needs) will be met only within the sect. Outside all is illusion or darkness or sin: inside is reality and light and liberty.

The other sects are more cautiously exclusive. Transcendental Meditation disclaims any religious basis (a claim which will be disproved later) and maintains that it is simply passing on a technique. Similarly, Scientology sets great store by its techniques, though it states clearly that it operates within a specific philosophical and religious framework which takes account of what all religions have been feeling after for thousands of years. The Hare Krishna movement urges people to find their way to God by what it believes to be the only true way, that of Krishna consciousness. Although these three are fairly cautious in the way they express their claims and although Scientology and Transcendental Meditation teach that their members may continue happily within the religion of their upbringing, it quickly becomes clear to anyone studying all three that they also are making exclusive claims and asking for total commitment.

All seven sects either teach or imply that real salvation is to be found only by becoming a member and thus accepting the beliefs, adopting the practices, or using the techniques therein prescribed.

Sometimes Christian churches or groups have adopted a similar stance. Some evangelicals of thirty or forty years ago implied that real Christianity was impossible unless certain taboos were observed. Even today within some circles it is implied that the 'real' Christian, or at any rate the 'full' and 'complete' Christian, is one who belongs to a particular group, or who can point to certain prescribed experiences, or who exhibits specific gifts.

All such claims, whether from within mainstream Christianity or from one of the sects, should be heard as danger signals. Fundamentally, Christian faith is not the acceptance of philosophical or theological dogmas, nor does it depend only upon spiritual experiences. Christian faith is trust in the Lord Jesus Christ as Saviour. Although Christians will wish to speak of the uniqueness of *Christ*, therefore, and of the exclusiveness of the claims *he* makes, they will nevertheless avoid identifying Christ and his claims exclusively with their own Christian group and its interpretation of the gospel. Church history and the more recent history of religious sects abound with examples of the pitfalls when such a stance is adopted.

Group superiority

The exclusiveness of sect claims lead in turn to the belief that the sect is an élite group. Because of its members' experience of the knowledge, grasp of the truth, or use of the techniques, those members are led to believe that they are distinct from, and superior to, those outside their membership. In some sects this distinction is recognized and fostered by the use of special terms to describe members or outsiders. Members of the Divine Light Mission, for example, are 'premies' and those given the guru's authority to pass on the experience to others are called 'mahatmas'. On the other hand, whereas those who have linked up with Sun Myung Moon's Unification Church are regarded as members of the Perfect Family, those outside the fellowship of the Family of Love are labelled 'systemites' because they are regarded as part of a God-rejecting materialistic system. Again, Scientology describes those with hang-ups in their sub-conscious as 'pre-clears', whereas those who have passed through this sect's processing to freedom from all inhibitions are called 'clears'.

These special terms, and the feeling of superiority lying behind them and encouraged by them, help to foster one of a religious sect's most important assets, strong group consciousness. Some of those who have left mainstream Christian churches to become members of sects have claimed that this is one of the chief attractions of the sect of their choice. In their sect they have found a group that is on the one hand strongly supportive, and which on the other hand makes them feel important as individuals. As we shall see later, strong pressures can build up within the group and this can lead to a repression of individuality, but there is little doubt that many waverers are persuaded to become fully committed sect members because of this strong sense of belonging which the sect provides. In some of the sects, the sense of group identity is further strengthened by the opposition which comes from 'unbelievers': indeed, sometimes sects seem to welcome and even encourage feelings of persecution for this reason.

There is no doubt that mainstream Christians have some important lessons to learn from the sects at this point. We need to rediscover, and where necessary recreate, the local church as the caring community, where people are free to be themselves and yet are able to encourage one another as disciples of Christ. We need to cultivate that warmth of fellowship which was a mark of the first-century church where 'all who believed were together and had all things in common',[8] and where there was a quality of informal worship and group consciousness often hard to detect in the mainstream churches today.

There are, of course, dangers to avoid. The fellowship can become so 'precious' that outsiders cannot survive in its atmosphere. The group can become so inward-looking that outsiders are never welcome. Cliques may develop, as they did in the Corinthian church in Paul's day. The main danger, however, appears to be in the opposite direction, with churches failing to cultivate the feeling of 'togetherness' often evident in the sects (and in many non-religious organizations), and with members remaining cold and aloof from one another. When this happens, it is hardly surprising that some people prefer to join the sects.

[8] Acts 2:44, RSV.

Strict discipline

Another common characteristic of the sects in this book is the strict discipline which they exert over their members. Usually that discipline takes the form of a rigid control over almost every aspect of members' lives, so that they have little time for anything other than the activities of the sect. The daily routine of life within the Family of Love, the Divine Light Mission, the Hare Krishna movement and the Unification Church provides typical examples. Members may also be required to submit their mail for censorship, to allow their leaders to decide which clothes they are to wear, or (as in the case of the Hare Krishna movement) even to allow their spiritual superiors to decide when they are to enjoy sexual intercourse with their married partners. Or the discipline may take the form of a heavy timetable of devotional or meditational requirements or many hours of missionary activities. No matter what demands are made, however, sect members are expected to obey their leaders without question. Some sects even teach their members that such obedience is required even when they know that their superiors are wrong.

Members stepping out of line are left in no doubt as to the wrongfulness of their disobedience. The rebuke may be relatively mild, with the strong hint that the action will not be tolerated again, or, as in the Church of Scientology, sanctions may be imposed to bring the culprit into line. Above all, however, there is the strong pressure of the group itself, and this ensures that on the whole members do what is required of them.

Such discipline can be very attractive when viewed alongside the flabbiness, overtolerance and indiscipline of much that today goes under the name of Christianity. Indeed, there is evidence that many people, especially young people, have become dissatisfied and disillusioned with the low demands that mainstream churches make on their members and are ready to respond positively to the challenge of a group which presents clear-cut standards and makes uncompromising demands.

Repression of individuality

Because there is no room for rebels within a sect, much of the training, especially of new recruits, aims to repress a member's individuality. This is particularly obvious in the Family of Love, for example, where members are affirming a creedal statement as they sing 'You've gotta be a baby', but to some extent the attitude is characteristic of most of the sects. Members surrender personal responsibility and place themselves unreservedly into the hands of their superiors. They must not think for themselves and must engage in no activity without the prior consent of those above them. There is no room for freedom of thought, difference of interpretation or independence of action. Members must not be themselves but must conform to a given stereotype.

Although Christ's words about being converted and becoming as little children are often used to justify this attitude, it is quite clear that the effects can be debilitating in the extreme. Worried parents of recruits often speak of their children as suffering changes of personality.

Doctrinal deviations

We began this chapter with Bryan Wilson's definition of sects as movements of religious protest. One very obvious form in which that protest expresses itself is in the rejection of many of the beliefs which mainstream Christianity regards as fundamental. Of the seven sects examined in succeeding chapters, three make specific claims to be Christian, three others derive many of their ideas from Hinduism, and the seventh provides an interesting attempt to combine the ideas of various religions and philosophies with some of the fantasies of science fiction. In this brief chapter, no attempt is being made to do anything more than state those general areas of belief in which deviations occur, for many of these important divergences will be considered in detail in later chapters. It will be helpful at the outset, however, to notice that although each of the sects differs widely from the others, together they share four very significant deviations from mainstream Christianity.

Authority

One of the most crucial questions to face in any religious discussion is that of authority, and this is certainly true with regard to the sects and Christianity. Christians are clear that ultimate authority resides in God alone, that God has revealed himself decisively in Jesus Christ, his incarnate Son, and that we learn all that we need to know of God and his will for our lives as we listen to the incarnate Word (Christ) speaking through the written word (the Bible). For us, therefore, Christian faith is biblical faith. Some of the sects in this book make the same claim, going so far as to maintain that their views come directly from the Bible.

As we shall see, however, they then add to the Bible a human source of authority, by claiming that the only legitimate interpretation of the Bible is that propounded by their leader or within their organization. Some of the other sects with which we are concerned have no hesitation in claiming another authoritative source in addition to, or instead of, the Bible. In both cases, however, the practical result is the same. The plain message of the Bible is added to, or altered, by the sect concerned. This is a clear departure from mainstream Christianity.

God

It is not surprising to find that, having rejected the authority of the Bible in matters of faith, the sects propound views of God that are far different from the picture of God derived from Jesus Christ and set out in the Bible. In those sects with a Christian background, this generally takes the form of a rejection of the idea of God as Trinity. In Hindu sects, God is seen in terms of the Hindu galaxy of gods, or impersonally, or sometimes (paradoxically) as a combination of the two. Whatever views are put forward, however, because they are not measured against the yardstick of the clear teaching of the Bible, they involve a repudiation of the doctrine of the Trinity.

Christ

Invariably, with the rejection of the Trinity, the sects deny the essential deity and eternity of Christ as Son of God.

19

With the Hindu-type sects, he may be recognized as one manifestation of the divine alongside many others. With the allegedly Christian sects, he becomes a special human being who, more than any other human being, shows us what God is like. These are very clear deviations from the mainstream Christianity of the historic creeds and formularies, where deity and humanity are seen to be held together in their fullness in the unique God-man.

Salvation

All the sects propound, in one way or another, salvation through human effort, which may take the form of submitting to certain rites or ceremonies, engaging in prescribed activities, or achieving required experiences. Whatever method is adopted, one thing is clear: the sects require people to save *themselves*.

In contrast, the Bible is clear that God sent his Son to be the Saviour of the world, that Jesus achieved salvation by offering himself as a sacrifice for our sins on the cross, and that we obtain salvation, not through our own efforts, but by accepting it as a free gift held out to us in the person of Jesus in whom we put our trust.

2. The Worldwide Church of God

'What has happened will happen again, and what has been done will be done again, and there is nothing new under the sun.' So wrote the Preacher in Ecclesiastes 1:9 centuries ago. Though Christians would hardly regard his words as an adequate encouragement for Christian progress, anyone who has studied the sects with which this book and its predecessor are concerned will wish to echo the Preacher's sentiments when it comes to the evaluation of the sects. Gnosticism, Arianism, Pelagianism and several other isms, all of which first appeared in the early days of Christianity, have reappeared constantly throughout the history of the Christian church. During the last two centuries they have been resuscitated in one form or another in modern sects.[1] When it comes to heresy, therefore, 'there is nothing new under the sun'.

Herbert W. Armstrong and his Worldwide Church of God are no exception. All of it has been said and done before. Despite the disclaimer by Armstrong's biographer that 'there was never any association in any way with Jehovah's Witnesses, Seventh-day Adventists, Mormons, or any such sects',[2] anyone familiar with such movements will soon detect close similarities in Armstrong's ideas. In particular, a Seventh-day Adventist writer has produced well-documented evidence that Armstrong was closely as-

[1] Werner Stark, *The Sociology of Religion*, vol. 2 (Routledge & Kegan Paul, 1969).
[2] Cited by W. R. Martin, *The Kingdom of the Cults* (Marshall, Morgan & Scott, 1967), p. 304.

sociated with a Seventh-day Adventists' splinter group in his early days.[3]

The founder of the Worldwide Church of God

Like most founders of modern religious sects, Herbert W. Armstrong (born in Des Moines, Iowa, USA, in 1892) was brought up in orthodox Christian circles. He says that as a boy he was a member of a 'respectable Protestant Church of traditional Christianity'.[4] It seems that after early association with the Quakers, he joined the Methodists. He found that his religion lacked reality, however, being orthodox but nominal, a matter of 'mere belief'. He accepted ideas of God and Christ as they were presented in mainstream Christianity and believed that salvation was all of faith and that works were unimportant. At this early stage of his life, however, most of his time and energy were devoted to his business rather than to his religion. He managed to build up a successful advertising agency in Iowa and looked set for a profitable career. During the 1920s, however, his hopes were shattered when his business crashed, though he and his followers are quick to point out that the collapse was through no fault of his.

Religion then began to be increasingly important to him, largely through the influence of his wife. A Seventh-day Adventist neighbour had persuaded her that obedience to God's spiritual law summed up in the Ten Commandments was necessary for salvation. Sin was the transgression of God's law, so one had to repent by turning from such transgression and by obeying God as a prior condition to salvation. Because such ideas ran counter to all that Armstrong had learnt in his 'respectable Protestant Church of traditional Christianity', about salvation being a free gift of God, his wife's new ideas led to some friction in the Armstrong household. Indeed, Armstrong was so incensed that he decided to make a careful study of the Bible to demonstrate that the Christian churches could not be

---

[3] *Ibid.*
[4] *The Plain Truth*, February 1973.

wrong and to point out to Mrs Armstrong the error of her ways. Far from discrediting her, however, he reached the conclusion that the Bible supported his wife's unorthodox views.

This was the turning-point of his religious life, his conversion. Very soon he began doing evangelistic work and in 1931 he was ordained into the ministry of the Church of God, a small denomination which observed Saturday as the holy day of the week. It was not long before he quarrelled with his new ministerial colleagues, however, and on the first Sunday of 1934 he began what was to become the Worldwide Church of God with a radio broadcast and the publication of a magazine.

Armstrong operates from Pasadena, California, where he founded the first of his Ambassador Colleges and started *The Plain Truth* magazine. He was quick to see the opportunities presented by broadcasting, and now claims that more than 50 million people listen to his broadcasts each week from over 300 radio stations throughout the world, and that a hundred television stations carry his programmes in the United States and Canada. More than two million copies of *The Plain Truth* are distributed free of charge each month. Readers of this well-produced glossy magazine, which contains well-written articles on current events, are also introduced to Armstrong's religious ideas and are encouraged to write to the movement for further literature. In recent years, shortage of money seems to have hit this institution, in common with most others, and there have been some cutbacks. Nevertheless the Worldwide Church continues to distribute much free literature and provides free Bible correspondence courses to any who write for them. 80,000 people are said to use such courses each month.

Herbert W. Armstrong's son, Garner Ted, has been prominent in his father's church for many years and at one time it seemed certain that he would eventually succeed to the leadership. Not only had he proved himself completely loyal to his father, but also he had taken on responsibility for most of the church's broadcasting. In 1972, however, there came a break between father and son over some undisclosed matter, and it seemed as if Herbert's plans for his son were not to be realized. Four months later, however, the two were reconciled, and Garner Ted is now once again active in the movement. But Herbert W. Armstrong himself remains firmly in control, and in his old age seems to have lost none of his drive.

The beliefs of the Worldwide Church of God

Like Jehovah's Witnesses, Christadelphians and others, Armstrong and his followers claim to base their teaching entirely upon the Bible. Unlike other sects such as Mormons, Christian Scientists and the Unification Church, they do not claim any additional revelation of divine truth, though they do claim that the mainstream Christian churches have departed from the clear teaching of the Bible. One of their most prolific writers asks, 'What was the teaching of Jesus Christ? The only authoritative answer is found in the inspired record of what Jesus did teach and in the perfect example He set for us to follow. Your own Bible contains this inspired record.'[5] As in any sectarian movement, however, the particular interpretations of the Bible favoured by the founder (especially when the founder is still alive) carry a lot of weight. In the case of Armstrong, he claims that the mainstream church has been in apostasy since AD 70 and that the plain truth was not restored until he began teaching it in the 1930s. This is a familiar story, for it is the same claim made (in one form or another) by most of the sects that hover around the perimeter of Christianity.

Nevertheless, the sect does claim to recognize the inspiration and authority of the Bible as the Word of God, and for that Christians will be glad. Here, at least, there is common ground. Unfortunately, as we shall see, some of the basic doctrines accepted by Christians because they are Bible-based are the very things which Armstrong and his followers seem to delight in rejecting.

[5] R. C. Meredith, in *The Plain Truth*, March 1973.

God and the Trinity
Armstrong rejects the view of orthodox Christianity that
God has revealed himself to us as Father, Son and Holy
Spirit, three Persons and one God. He asserts that those
who think of God as Trinity are as wrong as those who
think of God as one Person. He also believes that the idea
of the Spirit as the third Person of the Trinity is a 'heretical
and false doctrine introduced by pagan prophets'. The
whole Trinity doctrine is wrong, he believes, because 'it
limits God to three Persons' whereas God is much more.[6]

Noting that the Hebrew word for God, *Elohim*, is plural,
he prefers to interpret it as 'the Family of God'. Within this
divine family, God the Father and his Son have pride of
place, for they are 'the two original Beings in the God
Family',[7] but they are not alone. 'At the time of the resurrection we shall be instantaneously changed from mortal
into immortal – we shall then be born of God – we shall
then be God . . . You will actually be God, even as Jesus
was and is God, and His Father, a different Person, also is
God . . . You are setting out on a training to become creator
– to become God'.[8]

Such views make it hard to escape the conclusion that,
like Mormons, Armstrong and his followers think that the
difference between God and human beings is simply one of
degree. The Father and his Son are the original God-beings,
but those who follow Armstrong's teaching will join them
in the Godhead at the resurrection. There is no essential
difference between the Creator and his creatures: indeed,
creatures will one day become Creator. Commenting on
such views, W. R. Martin writes:

> The followers of Armstrong's cult should consult the
> third chapter of Genesis where they will find that Satan
> first taught the 'God family' doctrine to Adam and Eve.
> Both Armstrong and the Mormons have received and
> believed the same perversion which ushered in the reign

---

[6] Herbert W. Armstrong, *Just What Do You Mean – Born Again?*, pp. 17ff.
[7] Herbert W. Armstrong, *Tomorrow's World*, April 1971.
[8] Herbert W. Armstrong, *Why Were You Born?*, pp. 21ff.

of sin and death upon the human race, for if Satan lied when he said 'you shall be as gods' (verse 5) so does Mr Armstrong 'wrest the scripture to his own destruction' and sadly to the destruction, spiritually speaking, of those who follow in his training.[9]

Jesus Christ

Armstrong and his adherents affirm their belief in Christ's deity and eternity. 'He who had existed from eternity – He by whom God created the worlds and all things therein – He who was and is life – He who was made flesh – converted into flesh', is a typical statement about Christ.[10] On the other hand, they are so anxious to stress the reality of Christ's humanity while on earth that at times they get very near to the Jehovah's Witnesses' idea that while he was on earth Jesus was a perfect human being – no more and no less. Thus they state, 'The only difference between Jesus and any other human is that He was conceived of the Holy Spirit. Therefore He obeyed God's law from birth – and never had to go through the process of repenting of going the wrong way'.[11]

Though rejoicing in the reality of Christ's humanity as well as his full deity, Christians will wish to stress the uniqueness of their Lord, as Paul does in his great Christological hymn in Philippians 2:5–11. He who has existed from all eternity with his Father, as God, also became man. He did not cease to be God, but ceased to be treated as God. So in Christ we have a unique Person, one who combines in himself perfect Godhood and perfect humanity. Paul gives us, then, the New Testament pattern of Christ's history: pre-existence, incarnation, life, death, resurrection and ascension. These are the great historical realities upon which the Christian faith is based and without which it is non-existent. The question we have to ask of Armstrong and his Worldwide Church of God is this: To what extent are these New Testament truths set forth in your teachings?

In addition to their overstress on Christ's humanity al-

[9] W. R. Martin, op. cit., p. 314.
[10] The Plain Truth, April 1963.
[11] The Plain Truth, November 1963.

ready noted, with its tendency to devalue his deity, there are grave weaknesses in their interpretation of Christ's death and resurrection. Christians believe that when Christ died on the cross he was bearing the sin of the world and that when a person puts his faith in Christ that person's sins are forgiven, he is reconciled to God, he is born again, and he receives God's gift of eternal life. Christians further believe that when God raised his Son from the dead, he was not only vindicating his Son's claims and demonstrating the reality of life after death, but also assuring those with eyes to see that forgiveness and new life were possible through faith in Christ. No one can read the New Testament without realizing that the death and resurrection of Jesus are the heart of the Christian gospel. It follows that anyone who detracts from these central truths distorts that gospel.

It is disturbing to read, therefore, what Armstrong writes about Christ's death.

> The blood of Christ does not finally save any man. The death of Christ merely paid the penalty of sin in our stead – it wipes the slate clean of past sins – it saves us merely from the death penalty – it removes that which separates us from God and reconciles us to God.[12]

At this point there seems little to choose between Armstrong, Jehovah's Witnesses and Mormons. The three sects may express the idea in slightly different ways, but there is no doubt about its implication. Our hope lies, not solely in what Christ has done on our behalf, but on what we may achieve by our own efforts. All of this is far removed from Paul's teaching that 'by grace you have been saved through faith; and this is not your own doing, it is the gift of God – not because of works'.[13]

Armstrong's view of Christ's resurrection is equally inadequate. Orthodox Christians believe that the risen Christ has a real, though transformed, body – a body which in

[12] Herbert W. Armstrong, *All About Water Baptism*, p. 18.
[13] Ephesians 2:8–9, RSV.

some sense has a real continuity with his pre-resurrection body. The alternatives to this view are either that only the spirit of Christ survived (which does less than justice to the New Testament records), or that there was no real continuity between the human Jesus and the risen Christ. Armstrong chooses the second of these errors.

'God the Father', he tells us, 'did not cause Jesus Christ to get back into the body which had died.'[14] All that there was of Jesus died on the cross. Nothing remained. The Word had been made flesh. The eternal God, or at least that second Person of the God-family we know as Jesus Christ, had been changed into a human being of flesh and blood. He was not just an immortal spirit in a body of flesh and blood. This Jesus Christ really did die. He became non-existent. Then God raised him. But,

> The resurrected body was no longer human – it was the Christ resurrected, immortal, once again changed. As He had been changed, converted into mortal human flesh and blood, subject to death, and for the purpose of dying for our sins, now, by a resurrection from the dead, He was again changed, converted into immortality – and He is alive forevermore.[15]

Again, Armstrong is following hard on the heels of Jehovah's Witnesses. For, as I pointed out in *Some Modern Faiths*, the Witnesses have really divided Christ's existence into three chronological phases, each of which amounts to a complete existence in itself. So Jehovah's Witnesses believe Christ pre-existed in heaven as a spirit being, he was born on earth as a human being (no more and no less), and he was raised as a spirit being. Like Armstrong, therefore, they deny the bodily resurrection of Jesus Christ. I have not seen any of Armstrong's writings which spell out the implications quite as clearly as do Watch Tower publications, but there is little doubt that at this point Armstrong and the Witnesses believe the same thing. Like Jehovah's Witnesses, therefore, Armstrong and his follow-

---

[14] *The Plain Truth*, April 1963.   [15] *Ibid.*

ers are left with a problem. If all that there was of the earthly Jesus ceased to exist when he died, and there was no spirit or soul to survive even, what was it that God raised?

Already we have seen enough of Armstrong's views to be aware of the fact that he does not believe that Christ's death on our behalf is the ground of salvation and that by faith we accept salvation as the free gift of God offered to us in Christ. He agrees that the plan of salvation was *begun* on the cross, but he will not allow that Christ's death achieved that full salvation in which Christians have always rejoiced.

Armstrong spells out his views by making a careful distinction (unsupported by the Greek text of the New Testament) between *begettal* and *new birth*. We are *begotten* by God, he asserts, when we are converted; that is, when we repent, believe and begin to obey God's commandments. We are *born again*, he claims, not in this life but at the final resurrection at the second coming of Christ when we (that is, those who follow Armstrong's scheme of salvation) shall become immortal and part of the God-family.

There is no guarantee, however, that everyone begotten of God will be born again. All who are thus begotten of God have the potential to be born again, but whether they achieve what is possible will depend upon their obedience to God's commandments in the intervening period. So, as Mrs Armstrong first pointed out to her husband, 'Obedience to God's spiritual laws summed up in the Ten Commandments is necessary for salvation.' Such obedience (as we should expect from one who was greatly influenced by Seventh-day Adventism in his early years) includes the strict observance of a seventh-day sabbath, the honouring of Jewish holy days, and abstention from certain 'unclean' foods. On the other hand, the observance of Christian festivals, such as Christmas and Easter, is forbidden. Walter Martin is justified, therefore, when he describes the movement as 'the new Galatianism' and says,

> Mr Armstrong attaches to salvation the requirement of 'keeping the law and commandments of God'. This can only be described as adding to the gospel of grace the

conditions of law-keeping, the first-century heresy scathingly denounced in the Galatian epistle as 'another gospel' by no less an authority on the law than St Paul.[16]

Exclusivism

Along with most sects that have rejected mainstream Christianity, Armstrong and his followers believe that they alone have the truth and that every Christian denomination and every other sect is in error. Armstrong believes that after AD 70 'ministers of Satan' wormed their way into the church, branded as heretics the true people of God (*i.e.* those who shared the views he now teaches), and distorted the gospel. So 'for eighteen and one-half centuries that Gospel was preached. The world was deceived into accepting a false gospel.'[17] Then Armstrong appeared with the restored truth in the 1930s.

The 'official' church, however, remains in apostasy (he contends), for it has refused to accept Armstrongism.

> The entire apostate family – mother, and more than 500 daughter denominations, all divided against each other and in confusion of doctrines, yet all united in the chief pagan doctrines and festivals – has a family name. They call themselves 'Christian', but God calls them something else – 'Mystery, Babylon the Great'.[18]

Much could be written concerning Armstrong's claims at this point. We could remind ourselves, for example, that among the first 'ministers of Satan' who 'wormed their way into the church' with a distorted gospel were his own first-century predecessors, the Judaizers. They tried to do exactly what Armstrong attempts, to add to the gospel of grace certain legalistic extras as necessary to salvation. Those familiar with Paul's writings will know what the apostle thought of them and their teaching. Again, we could consider the strangeness (not to say the arrogance) of the

---

[16] W. R. Martin, *op. cit.*, p. 319.
[17] *The Inside Story of the World Tomorrow Broadcast*, pp. 7ff.
[18] *Easter is Pagan*, pp. 8–9.

claim that there was no real gospel preaching from AD 70 until Armstrong appeared with his message in the 1930s. Or we could remind ourselves that despite all its diversity and disunity, the mainstream Christian church which Armstrong so obviously despises is united in its acceptance of those basic doctrines which were preached in the apostolic church and have been preached throughout the church's history. There is an apostolic succession (in the handing on of the Christian deposit of truth) that disproves what Armstrong claims.

Anglo-Israelism

Others have expounded the theory of Anglo-Israelism in detail.[19] Briefly it states that the ten tribes, 'lost' when the Assyrians conquered Israel and brought the Northern Kingdom to an end, are now to be found in the Anglo-Saxons, found largely in Britain and the USA. All the covenant promises made to Israel in the Old Testament, it is asserted, now apply to these two countries, Britain being identified with Ephraim and the USA with Manasseh. The Jews, on the other hand, are identified with Judah and remain under the divine curse. One of the key ideas of Anglo-Israelism is the belief that the throne of David is now the throne of England.

We shall not attempt to discuss the many arguments that may be levelled against these strange views. This has been done many times by other authors. It is enough to say that reputable Bible scholars do not support the very strange exegesis of biblical texts necessary to equate Great Britain and the USA with the lost ten tribes of Israel, or to identify the throne of England with that of King David. Armstrong is not the first to put forward such views, however, and within orthodox Christian churches there are some people who would make similar claims.

Anglo-Israelism does not in itself make a movement heretical, of course, even though many people would argue that such views are not supported in any way by the Bible. Enough has been stated in this brief chapter to show, how-

[19] *E.g.* W. R. Martin, *op. cit.*, pp. 295ff.

ever, that even if we ignore this aspect of Armstrong's teaching the Worldwide Church of God's views about God, Christ and salvation are so removed from biblical Christianity as to condemn the views of Armstrong and his followers as heretical.

Summary of main differences

Armstrong	*Christianity*
God	
The divine family includes, not only God the Father and his Son, but also ultimately all who follow Armstrong's teaching and are obedient to the divine commandments.	There is one God, yet within the unity of the Godhead there are three divine Persons, the Father, the Son and the Holy Spirit.
Man	
All human beings are potentially God the Creator.	Though made in God's image and promised a glorious future with their heavenly Father, believers remain God's creatures.
Salvation	
Christ's death on the cross did not achieve man's salvation, but gave everyone the opportunity of a fresh start. We are now free to earn our salvation by obeying God's commandments.	Achieved by Christ, who died and rose again for us, salvation is not something we earn but God's gift to be appropriated through faith. 'For it is by his grace you are saved, through trusting him; it is not your own doing. It is God's gift, not a reward for work done' (Ephesians 2:8–9).

Resurrection

The bodily resurrection of Jesus is denied. Christ's resurrection was in effect a recreation.

The resurrection of Jesus is affirmed as a real historical event involving the same Jesus in bodily form.

Church

The true church consists of those who accept Armstrong's teachings. The so-called churches of Christendom are apostate.

The one church consists of all the people of God, those who through faith have accepted Jesus as Saviour and acknowledge him as Lord.

Sabbath

Saturday is a legally binding sabbath, as set out in the Old Testament.

Sunday is observed as a thankful and joyful remembrance of Christ's resurrection.

Israel

Britain and the United States of America are the 'lost tribes' of Israel and the British monarch is a descendant of King David.

The church is the true Israel, so now 'there is no such thing as Jew and Greek, slave and freeman, male and female; for you are all one in Christ Jesus' (Galatians 3:28).

3 The Family of Love

The Family of Love, still better known under its former name, The Children of God, grew out of the wider Jesus Movement which originated in the USA in the 1960s. It needs to be pointed out, however, that members of this sect are not simply evangelical Christians who have rejected conventional church life and dropped out of western society – which is what they would like us to believe. Rather, they are part of a notorious organization that has been responsible for the break-up of families and which encourages its members to practise sexual immorality in the name of religion.

As the Children of God, this sect was founded by David Berg, one-time Christian minister, who began calling himself Moses David and who wrote Mo-letters instructing his followers what to believe and how to behave. His followers came to regard Berg as God's special prophet for the twentieth century, a divinely appointed envoy whose task was to call people to repent. The particular form of repentance required included the rejection of the churches of Christendom which, so Berg taught, had turned their backs on Christ, as predicted in the book of Revelation, and had become part of the great whore of Babylon.

Because they sprang from the Jesus Movement and were the first representatives of that movement to make an impact in Britain, it is necessary to look briefly at that wider movement. In particular, it is important to try to understand what they have in common with the Jesus People and where they differ widely from them.

The Jesus Movement

Opinions differ as to how the Jesus Movement began, though most people agree that no one Christian leader can be given sole credit for it. Many would say, however, that in the early stages the movement owed much to Ted Wise. In 1966, as a drug-taking sailmaker living near San Francisco, Wise came across a Bible, read it and was converted to Christ. Thrilled with his new life-transforming experience, he began sharing the gospel with his friends and contacts, and after a few months had been used to lead many of them to Christ. Wise and his converted friends then set up a coffee-bar type of evangelistic enterprise, and through this activity hundreds of young people were converted over the next two years. If this was not actually the beginning of the Jesus Movement, it was certainly a clear indication that the Holy Spirit was beginning to work through unusual channels among the drug addicts and drop-outs in American youth culture.

As Micheal Jacob has pointed out, it is probably true that the name 'Jesus Movement' 'is one of those phrases that journalists invent to describe a phenomenon which they do not wholly understand, . . . It is an imprecise phrase, covering a wide spectrum of people and organizations and incorporating many viewpoints.'[1] In other words, it is a useful piece of shorthand, pointing to a movement of world-renouncing young Christians who, having been converted to Christ (often in a dramatic manner from a background of drug addiction), overflow with Christian love, emphasize the importance of both fellowship and evangelism, and look for the return of Christ within their own lifetime. These 'Jesus freaks', as some call them, see little point in working within the kind of society surrounding them in the western world, and have become Christian drop-outs. Enjoying each other's company, they often live in Christian communes and happily share their scanty belongings with one another. Because of the manner in which they have become Christians and the way in which they

---

[1] Micheal Jacob, *Pop Goes Jesus* (Mowbray, 1972), p. 16.

understand their faith, they are very rarely attracted by the conventional Christian churches, though in America a few unconventional Christian ministers, notably Arthur Blessitt, have found a welcome among them.

Most of them believe that American Christianity has tried to control Christ rather than to allow him to revolutionize it. They point out that conventional Christians do not readily talk about Christ in a natural way and do not apply Christ's teaching to their lives. There are perhaps more than 300,000 young people within the Jesus Movement in the United States. Inevitably, their impact has been felt among Christians in many other parts of the world and there can be little doubt that much of the informality and renewed vitality currently seen in some of the churches in Britain owe as much to the Jesus Movement as to the Charismatic Movement. It is worth noticing, however, that by and large the British equivalent of the Jesus Movement has been making its presence felt within the conventional churches rather than outside them. Moreover, some Christian leaders in Britain, including one or two of the bishops of the Established Church, have welcomed the Jesus People as a valuable revitalizing influence within their more traditional congregations.

By and large, the Jesus Movement is characterized by a willingness of its members to share their property with one another, following the example of Acts 2; by a staunchly fundamentalist attitude to the Bible; and by a simple lifestyle. Members are not very concerned about church buildings but are happy to meet for worship and evangelism anywhere, inside or out of doors. They have little time for theology and theologians (even those which reflect their own evangelical beliefs); and, on the whole, although they care for one another's needs, they make little attempt to apply their beliefs to social issues outside their immediate fellowship. Many of them have a rather simplistic and unscriptural view that when a person becomes a real Christian all his problems disappear. Musically, they prefer pop, and Jesus tents are usually in evidence at pop festivals, where those attending are offered free food and literature accompanied by personal testimony for Christ. Speaking in tongues, healings and other Pentecostal elements are emphasized.

Although we have been describing the Jesus Movement, it is important to remember that it is not a unified movement in the sense that it possesses any kind of organizational cohesion. It also contains wide diversities of belief and practice within the general framework of the characteristics mentioned earlier. So, for example, whilst some Jesus people are happy to associate with Christians of the conventional churches, others claim not only that the conventional churches have sold the pass and that their members are not real Christians, but also that within the Jesus Movement itself only their own interpretation of the Christian faith is valid and that those who disagree with them are not really Jesus People at all.

This last view was that of David Berg, and on that basis he founded the Children of God. Berg has now apparently abdicated as leader, and, according to some people, has claimed that the movement he started was nothing more than a hoax. But his followers, many of whom now prefer the name Family of Love, still believe his statement, 'You are the one and only real Jesus people.' The Children of God, alias the Family of Love, are without doubt the most revolutionary of the many groups that have emerged within the Jesus Movement: they have been described by the American magazine *Time* as 'the storm troopers of the Jesus revolution'. They are exclusivist, regarding themselves as the sole faithful, God-fearing remnant in a world that has rejected God. Other Jesus people are regarded as disobedient to God and lukewarm in their Christian commitment. As for the mainstream churches, they are regarded as worldly, half-hearted and completely hypocritical, and part of that system which God will soon destroy.

The founder of the Family of Love

David Berg, now about sixty years old, is a former American Baptist minister. His parents were full-time evangelists working with the American Christian and Missionary Alliance, and Berg spent much of his early life travelling widely with them in their work. He himself eventually became pastor of a church in Arizona, but after a dispute with his congregation he left them at the end of the second world war. Berg claims that it was because they refused to pay him enough to support a family of six, but they say he was dismissed because his work was unsatisfactory.

Berg, or Moses David as he prefers to be called, then moved on to South California, where he linked up with a Pentecostal minister named Fred Jordan. Jordan was working in radio ministry and had founded a pastoral counselling centre which he called a soul clinic. Berg joined him as his press officer for a short time, but then with his family and friends moved on once more. In 1968 he settled at Huntington Beach, where he ran a coffee house and wrote a book about his mother which he called *The Hem of His Garment*. This publication was highly regarded within the sect and was read alongside the Bible and Berg's other writings. He started a movement called Teens for Christ, based on the coffee house, establishing a communal pattern of life for his converts which included sessions of intensive Bible study. From the start he encouraged them to withdraw from their jobs and to drop out of society, which he taught them was an evil system. As founder of Teens for Christ, Berg began to display the authoritarian attitude to his followers that is a characteristic of the sect today and managed to instil into them a fanatical loyalty. The movement lasted only about a year, however, until in 1969 Berg prophesied that California was about to come under the judgment of God and after an earthquake would fall into the sea. He and his disciples decided to move on quickly and adopted a nomadic role.

It was from this point onwards that Berg and his followers began to call themselves the Children of God. After wandering for about eight months, they settled for a time on a ranch owned by Berg's former colleague, Fred Jordan, in Texas. Then in September 1971 Berg again broke with Jordan and moved further afield. In recent years, he has virtually become a recluse and is never seen in public, though his Mo-letters are still very much in evidence among his followers. As we have seen, he has now renounced his leadership. With or without his aid, however, the Family of Love have branched out into many parts of the world. Although their membership probably amounts to no more than 5,000 fully committed disciples living in some 830 colonies, they are known to many more people through their persistent attempts to sell their literature and to share their beliefs, and through the widespread (and sometimes adverse) publicity their activities have received.

As stated earlier, they were the first representatives of the much larger and diverse Jesus Movement to arrive in Britain. When they first appeared in London, they were sponsored by an evangelical businessman, Kenneth Frampton. Believing them to be a sincere group of evangelistically-minded young Christians, he allowed them to use one of his properties as their headquarters. After members of his own family joined the sect and he learnt at first hand more of their aims and methods, however, Frampton changed his mind and now says publicly,

> Having backed this movement more than any since they arrived in Britain, I repent for having encouraged the active propagation of what now proves to be false teaching, dishonouring to Christ.[2]

The beliefs of the Family of Love

The only real Christians
It is a fundamental belief of this sect that its members are the only true Christians, the only obedient servants of God at work in the world today. Outside the movement, they claim, everything is sinful, satanic, hypocritical and anti-Christian. In the extravagant language typical of the Mo-letters, David Berg wrote,

> Kids have been kidnapped from their homes by the laws of compulsory school attendance; drugged to damnation by modern, godless, and useless public education; hypnotized by TV, movies, magazines, and modern music;

[2] K. P. Frampton, *Beware – The Children of God*, p. 3.

39

and imprisoned by modern curfews, child labour laws, parental jurisdiction laws, minimum marriage age laws, minor's laws, and draft regulations and military bondage.[3]

The Family of Love believe that the mainstream Christian churches are every bit as anti-Christian as are other organizations which do not profess to be Christian.

> The fiendish, devilish economic system, we hate it, and we teach the kids to hate it, and the False Church system. . . . We hate the hypocrisy, self-righteousness, lies and deceitfulness of those who claim to be the Church, but are not and we hate the Spiritual system of the Devil behind them.[4]

Berg taught that the Children of God, despite their small numbers, had been called by God to fight on his side against everything evil and that everything outside the sect was part of the devil's system which had to be destroyed. Thus, all those involved in such an evil society were labelled 'systemites', and ought to be opposed at every turn.

This attitude prevails within the sect today and helps to encourage a persecution complex among members. Not only is every 'systemite' an enemy to be opposed in every possible way, but the Family of Love must be ready to suffer persecution at the hands of such people. Indeed, persecution is believed to prove that the sect is in the right, for all opposition demonstrates that the devil is taking it seriously. As in some other sects, persecution is almost welcomed and cultivated, for it helps to encourage a sense of group identity and dependence, making it all the more difficult for wavering members to make the necessary effort to break away.

David Berg described Jesus as the 'greatest of all Revolutionaries' and the apostles as 'His twelve bearded militants'[5] who fought with a 'commando-guerilla type of

---

[3] *Mo-letters*, cited by K. P. Frampton, *op. cit.*, p. 5.   [4] *Ibid.*

[5] Ron Harris, *Time Out*, 17–23 August 1973, citing 'Letters for Leaders'.

hit and run tactics'.[6] Similarly, the Children of God were to regard themselves as today's Christian revolutionaries. Taking up this theme, a journalist described members of the sect as 'David Berg's own private army, highly organized to follow his message from God'.[7] Being thus at war with society, members of the sect have always felt justified in adopting appropriate wartime tactics, such as the deliberate dissemination of lies and 'spoiling the Egyptians' (the phrase used to describe the actions whereby members get as much money and property as they can from those outside their ranks, the non-believing parents of converts being special targets in this respect).

The Bible and Berg's pronouncements
When they first appeared in Britain as the Children of God, the Family of Love seemed to be simple evangelical Christians with a love for the Scriptures which they claimed to regard as the inspired Word of God. Much of their energy was spent encouraging novices to learn biblical texts by heart. Outside the movement, however, this apparent loyalty to the Bible began to be seen in the light of the special place Berg himself occupied within the sect and the view of his writings and pronouncements which his followers held. Undoubtedly, the Children of God saw him as God's special messenger, the prophet for our time. He was their charismatic leader: they were his disciples or devotees. It followed that the only interpretation of the Bible allowed to members was that which Berg himself propounded. In practice, therefore, though lip-service was paid to the Bible, the real authority within the sect was David Berg. As Moses David he was God's mouthpiece, the true interpreter of Scripture and source of true religion.

It soon became clear, moreover, that as a twentieth-century prophet, Berg's role was not confined merely to interpreting Scripture. His followers obviously believed that in his published Mo-letters they had a continuation of the Bible for today. Indeed, God was said to be using Moses

[6] *Mo-letter*, November 1972, cited by Ron Harris, *op. cit.*
[7] Cited by Ron Harris, *op. cit.*

David to speak to the present generation just as he had used Isaiah, Jeremiah, Ezekiel and others to speak to previous generations. From the first, Christians rejected these claims, believing them to be either the meanderings of a man deluded by his own megalomania or the deliberate deceptions of a kind of religious confidence man. The second of these views appears to have been justified in the light of recent events.

At the time, however, the claim that Berg's writings were in some sense inspired made strange reading to those familiar with the Mo-letters. Not only were they written in a racy style and sometimes punctuated with foul language, but they contained a number of explicitly sexual images and in some places descriptions of the sex act itself. Former member, Aram Outim, has said, 'Sex is really an obsession with Moses'. In defence, Children of God claimed that their leader was merely emphasizing that sex, as a God-given gift, was something that people were meant to enjoy, not something of which they should be ashamed. But others found it difficult to accept that, in trying to make this point, Berg needed to go into great detail when describing, for example, his own sexual dreams. Many regarded his writings as pornographic. As we shall see, the prominence given to sex in Berg's writings has had practical repercussions in the sexual behaviour of the sect's members. Only time will tell whether, with the departure of Berg and its own development from the Children of God phase to its new phase as the Family of Love, the sect will still wish to regard the writings of its founder in the same way. There can be no doubt, however, that so far Berg's writings have been regarded in this sect as a special word from God.

The second coming and judgment
Among the Family of Love, there is a very strong expectation that Christ will soon return. The year 1993 has been mentioned as a possible date. This emphasis on an imminent second coming is a characteristic, not only of a number of the sects on the Christian perimeter, but also of many mainstream Christian groups, such as those affected by the Jesus Movement and the Charismatic Movement.

Unlike most orthodox Christians, however, the Family of Love are fairly specific about what is to happen when Christ returns. Not only do they speak in general terms about his return as Judge, but they go on to spell out what form the judgment will take and who will suffer under it. In particular, they expect severe punishment to be meted out to the churches of the western world and to the materialistic society in which they have worked and to which they have sinfully conformed. Because of this aspect of their message, they have been labelled as Jeremiah prophets.

They themselves expect to be fighting on God's side against a one-state government of Antichrist before the turn of the century. All the traditional churches of Christendom will then suffer under God's judgment because of their world-conformity and downright hypocrisy.

It is against this background that the sect calls people, especially young people, to turn their backs on the sinful world and to join God's army as Christ's revolutionaries. As we shall see, those successfully recruited are expected to forsake all, including their families, friends and jobs, since all other people are 'systemites' and all other activities are part of the world of the Antichrist.

The methods of the Family of Love

Much of the sect's evangelistic outreach in this country follows the traditional pattern of Christian evangelism, with public witnessing and the distribution of literature (which they call 'litnessing'). The Family of Love are, in practice, much more dedicated to this approach and persistent in it than are conventional Christians, however, members frequently spending up to ten hours a day distributing their pamphlets. They often work in public places such as shopping areas, and use songs in the folk-music vein to convey their ideas. Each member has a quota of pamphlets to sell and is expected to work for many hours each day to reach, or if possible to surpass, his target.

In the USA a more dramatic approach to outreach has included vigils. Members, as prophets of doom, wearing red sackcloth to denote the need to repent and with their foreheads daubed with ash as a sign of mourning, have paraded publicly with wooden yokes around their necks, symbolizing bondage, and wearing one ear-ring, as a sign that they are slaves of Christ. They carry wooden staves, signifying divine judgment. Dressed thus, they have been known to interrupt public ceremonies and to disrupt church services, proclaiming God's impending judgment upon American society and calling for repentance. William Petersen gives a vivid description of one incident:

> Once they marched into San Francisco's famed Grace Cathedral on top of Nob Hill. During the entire service they stood silently and forebodingly in the centre aisle; then at the close of the service they shouted 'Repent', in a unison voice that reverberated throughout the cathedral leaving the worshippers almost shell-shocked.[8]

The philosophy behind such action is made clear.

> We have declared War of the Spirit on the system's godless schools, Christless churches, and heartless Mammon! We long to return to the Truth, Love, Peace, and Beauty of our Ancients in dress, customs, appearance, and the simple Life of True Happiness in God and love for our fellow man.[9]

Such 'love' is much emphasized within the sect and has contributed very much to the attractiveness of the Family of Love to youngsters outside its ranks. Sect members are instructed to tell contacts, 'We believe in Jesus and we really love you.' It is all part of the 'love bombing' technique. Some members of the sect have taken it to its logical but antinomian extreme by offering free sex to outsiders, 'to show them the love of God'. They claim it is a form of witnessing. Members argue that 'Jesus taught that we should be willing to die for others. Surely, then, we ought

---

[8] William Petersen, *Those Curious New Cults* (Keats Publishing Inc., Connecticut, 1975), p. 152.

[9] Part of the statement signed by new recruits when joining the sect.

to be willing to give them sex.'[10]

In such ways, the Family of Love call young people to forsake all and follow Christ. The forsaking is expected to include their families and friends, and their jobs, all of which are included in the sinful 'system' of the devil which must be rejected. On the positive side, recruits are expected to join a colony and to allow every aspect of their life thereafter to be dictated to them by their leaders, the sect's shepherds. Some critics claim that such colonies exert a sinister, hypnotic spell on new converts. It is certainly true that because of the group pressures (or what the members themselves would describe as the support of the family), members find themselves prepared to do things that they never would have contemplated doing outside the sect.

The first stage in committed membership is that of a 'babe' in a kind of 'nursery', a special colony for novices. Here the main object will be to make the new recruit totally dependent upon the colony's leader. Like a natural baby, the novice must have no opinions of his own and must take no action of any kind that is not first ordered by the shepherd. He must go nowhere and do nothing without the permission of his superior. At this stage (and subsequently, for this total dependence continues beyond the novice stage), his theme song will be, 'You've gotta be a baby, to go to heaven.'

After the novice stage, the convert is moved to another place for more advanced teaching. There too he will find that the whole of his life revolves around the colony. He will be subjected to rigid discipline and will never be permitted to move outside the colony unless accompanied by another member. He will be discouraged from having too much contact with his parents; letters from him to them will be censored, and their letters to him will be read before he sees them. It was in response to such behaviour that in February 1972 in San Diego some worried American parents of Children of God converts, claiming that their children had been kidnapped, hypnotized and brainwashed,

---

[10] Members of the sect argued this in a BBC radio programme, 'The Lobster Pot', in the autumn of 1978.

set up FREECOG (Parents Committee to Free Our Sons and Daughters from the Children of God). The sect's response was to form a rival organization, THANKCOG, of parents who were said to be grateful to the sect for the wonderful changes wrought in their children, a number of whom were said to be former drug addicts rescued by the Children of God.

Despite the existence of the rival organizations, one thing is clear. Members are given specific instruction within the sect to wean them away from loyalty to unbelieving parents. The sect frequently quotes Matthew 10:34–37 in support of its attitude, pointing out that part of the sacrifice Jesus expected of his followers was their willingness to place their loyalty to him before every other loyalty, including that of family ties. They claim that they, unlike conventional Christians, take Christ at his word in this respect (as in every other) and are willing to make even this sacrifice for him.

A typical day in the life of a colony might run something like this. Members would be expected to rise fairly early. Much of the morning would then be spent in prayer, the memorizing of the Bible verses supplemented by key passages from Mo-letters, communal Bible study and housework. Then from about noon until 6 p.m., they would be sent out from the colony to witness to others and try to sell their movement's literature. Much of the sect's money is raised in this way, for it is not unusual to find members who each raise about £20 a day by this means. All of the money goes into the common purse. Dinner at 7 p.m. might be followed by an evening meeting with singing and testimonies. Then at about 10.30 p.m. 'lights out' would be announced and the members of the colony would settle down for a night's sleep.

Since David Berg's renunciation of the sect's leadership and apparent repudiation of all that it stands for has happened so recently, it is not possible to say what effect this will have on the patterns of leadership within the Family of God. Under Berg, the sect was theoretically a theocracy, with Berg serving as 'king' under God. The sect's strict discipline and authoritarianism stemmed directly from the leader. Following Berg's example, the Children of God were all given biblical names. This was said to be partly for security reasons, for they were expecting a communist take-over and were preparing themselves for life under a godless dictatorship when they as Christians would be persecuted. For similar reasons, an aura of mystery surrounded the supreme leader and those who occupied positions of authority under him. It was quite common to find that one colony had no contact with another colony, again for security reasons. Even before his recent renunciation, Berg was seen very rarely and lived in seclusion, but ensured that his wishes were carried out among his followers through a pyramidal authority structure that affected every part of the organization.

Immediately below Berg came his 'royal family', consisting of members of his immediate family and their partners. Then came the 'council of ministers', then twelve 'bishops' each of whom was responsible for one of the areas into which the sect had divided the world for missionary activities. Below the 'bishops', the work was overseen by 'regional shepherds', and each of these looked after a number of 'district shepherds'. Each 'district' had several 'colonies', and leading each 'colony' was a 'colony shepherd'.

No 'colony' was expected to have more than twelve members. As stated earlier, strict censorship was imposed within the colony and, except at times of organized outreach, there was little or no communication between those living within the colony and those on the outside. When a member joined a colony, he was expected to become totally committed and to hand over all his belongings. He signed a statement saying, 'I promise to give all my goods and income, to let you open my mail, and to obey rules and officers.' The handing over of property was justified by Acts 2:44–45. A disturbing feature of all of this was that the member was expected to try to obtain as much money as possible from relatives outside the sect.

It is early days to say whether such rigid control will persist now that Berg no longer leads the movement. The early 1980s will clearly demonstrate whether, with the demise of the founder, this sect will disintegrate (like many before it) or become an 'established' sect, after the pattern of Jehovah's Witnesses or Mormons.

The Family of Love and Christianity

In some respects, the Children of God/Family of Love are the most difficult of the sects examined in this book. As we have seen, they claim to base their teaching upon the Bible. They also say that they are fully committed to, and have a living experience of, Jesus Christ as Saviour and Lord. They do not openly reject cardinal Christian doctrines, as do the Divine Light Mission and the Unification Church. On the contrary, they use much of the traditional language of evangelical Christianity. Because of such factors, it is not so immediately obvious where they depart from mainstream Christianity. It is arguable that, with Berg at their head, their error was not so much that of rejecting orthodox Christianity wholesale as that of listening too much to the views of one man and allowing him to dictate how they were to interpret Scripture and therefore to determine their beliefs and practices. Their fundamental error, therefore, was the place they allowed David Berg to occupy at the centre of their organization and, therefore, the influence they allowed him to have over their beliefs and behaviour. They regarded his writings and pronouncements at least as the sole authoritative interpretations of Scripture, in this respect following hard upon the heels of Christian Scientists who have a similar view of Mary Baker Eddy's *Science and Health with Key to the Scriptures*. Like the Mormons, however, they then went further, treating Berg's writings (as the Mormons treated Smith's writings) as additional divine revelations through a present-day prophet and, therefore, as additional scriptures. To put it simply, though claiming to be a Bible-*only* group, they became a Bible-*plus* group, the 'plus' being in the form of David (Moses David) Berg.

By adopting such a stance, the Children of God (as they were then called) displayed one of the most obvious characteristics of religious sects, noted by such writers as the British sociologist Bryan Wilson and the Lutheran theologian Kurt Hutten: namely, the espousal of some different source of authority from that of mainstream Christianity. Taking as a picture the ordination of a Swedenborgian minister, who held a Bible in his right hand and a book written by Swedenborg in his left, Hutten asserts that every sect has 'a Bible in the left hand', that is, another source of authority which it uses to interpret, and often to supplement or supersede, the teaching of the Bible itself.[11] By allowing themselves slavishly to follow Berg's teachings, the Children of God also fell into this error. Then, having made that cardinal error, others inevitably followed. Briefly, we notice one or two.

Flying in the face of the clear and uncompromising teaching of the Bible about truthfulness, this sect, like the Unification Church, adopted the evil maxim that the end justifies the means. Thus deliberate lying and deceit became legitimate tools to be employed in producing the desired end, another recruit for the sect.

Then there is the distortion of the teaching of Jesus contained in Matthew 10:34–37, used to persuade converts to forsake their parents and break all family ties. It is obviously true that Jesus does demand a loyalty above all other loyalties. There may well be occasions (as most Christians discover) when even the wishes of those nearest and dearest to us have to take second place because of their conflict with what we understand to be the will of God for us. But this does not give the slightest justification for the view that, as an automatic consequence of becoming Christ's disciple, a young person must turn his back on the parents who reared him, pausing long enough only to collect from them as much of their money and as many of their possessions as he can persuade them to part with before he leaves. There are other scriptures stressing the importance of honouring one's parents and fostering one's family ties, such as Exodus 20:12 and Ephesians 6:1. It is significant that, in order to avoid the plain application of those verses, the Children of God needed Berg's special interpretation, namely that obeying your parents in fact

---

[11] Kurt Hutten, *Die Glaubenswelt des Sektierers*, p. 104, cited by A. Hoekema, *The Four Major Cults* (Paternoster, 1963), p. 378.

meant 'obeying your leadership, not your ungodly fleshly parents' and, what is more, obeying these leaders even when they were wrong. Needless to say, there is not the slightest justification for Berg's views. The context makes it quite clear that these verses are dealing with relationships within the natural family.

Berg's preoccupation with sex also needs some comment. It is true that the Christian church has not always recognized that sex is a gift of God, and if Berg had simply been trying to make that point many orthodox Christians would have agreed with him. Unfortunately, however, instead of stressing the wonder, beauty and sacredness of sexual relationships and the Bible's requirement that they should take place within the bond of marriage, Berg's approach can be described at best as coarse, and at worst as pornographic. That, allied with some evidence of what most people would regard as at least undue permissiveness and perhaps even promiscuity among his followers, leads one to ask whether this is the kind of behaviour that one would associate with a true prophet of God. It certainly falls a long way short of the Bible's standards for sexual morality.

So, by setting up a man as their final authority, by practising deceit to achieve their ends, by requiring their followers to break natural family ties, by promoting an unscriptural attitude to sex, and by enslaving their followers to a system rather than liberating them to serve Christ freely, the Children of God demonstrated that their claim to be the only true Christians was without the slightest foundation. That claim could have been justified only in the minds of those who were prepared to reject the clear teaching of Jesus and his apostles and to replace it with the alleged new truths of a discredited false prophet.

But now Berg has gone. It remains to be seen whether his erstwhile disciples are now ready to repudiate the anti-Christian views and practices he foisted upon them and become true 'Jesus people', or whether, under a different leadership, they will continue to demonstrate that they are anything but the children of God.

Summary of main differences

Family of Love | *Christianity*

Authority

David Berg is the twentieth-century prophet, God's authoritative spokesman to an evil world. He gives new truth and the only legitimate interpretation of the Bible.

God has revealed himself and his will for us in the Person and teaching of Christ, his incarnate Word. All that we know of Christ is contained in the Bible, the written Word. The Bible is the yardstick against which all claims to truth are to be measured, including those made by earthly leaders claiming a prophetic gift.

Church

They alone are the real Christians. All others, including members of the churches of Christendom, are of the devil.

The one Church consists of all the people of God, who through faith have accepted Jesus as Saviour and acknowledge him as Lord.

Second coming

Christ will return soon, possibly within the next decade.

Though a sure and certain hope is promised in the Bible, no-one knows the time of Christ's return.

Discipleship

Converts are expected to give up all freedom and independence and to become childishly dependent upon their spiritual superiors.

As disciples of Christ, Christians have been set free from every kind of bondage, have begun to experience fullness of life in Christ, and are expected to live mature lives as God's servants.

4 The Unification Church

Members of the Unification Church, commonly known as Moonies because they are the disciples of Sun Myung Moon, have become increasingly active in Britain during the last five years. Large gatherings in London and other large cities, publicity stunts throughout the United Kingdom, and widespread proselytizing activities by zealous adherents, to say nothing of adverse comments in the United States Congress and a number of court cases, have encouraged the media to draw the public's attention to Sun Myung Moon and his followers. Moreover, because this sect claims to be a movement aimed at the unification of world-wide Christianity, some members of mainstream Christian churches have been misled into thinking that the Moonies are their allies in a worthy cause. Members of the Unification Church, practising what they call 'heavenly deception', have fostered such thinking. It has been part of the Moonies' strategy to try to infiltrate Christian congregations. Some misguided Christians have even been known to allow Moonies to take over Christian acts of worship. On the other hand, the Archbishop of Canterbury and other prominent leaders of the mainstream Christian denominations have stated publicly that the Unification Church is not part of mainstream Christianity. The British Council of Churches has turned down the Unification Church's application for membership of the Council and has published a leaflet against its beliefs and practices.

The purpose of this brief examination is to inform readers about the history, beliefs and methods of the Moonies and to point out where their beliefs and practices differ from those of mainstream Christianity. Not that I have any reason to doubt the sincerity of those Moonies I have met and who have taken great pains to explain their religion to me. On the contrary, I believe that most of them are very sincere and, indeed, put many Christians to shame by their zealous attempts to spread their faith. In this respect they are like most of the adherents of all the sects examined in this book. But sincerity is not enough. Saul of Tarsus is a standing example of one who, until his conversion on the Damascus road, was sincerely wrong. It is because I believe the Moonies to be wrong and regard their teachings and their practices to be untrue and therefore un-Christian that I write this chapter.

The Unification Church's founder

Sun Myung Moon was born on 6 January 1920 in Jeongju, a small town in the north of Korea, as one of eight children raised by Presbyterian parents in rather humble circumstances. Moon claims that on Easter Day 1936, when he was 16 years old, he received the first of a series of direct divine revelations. Jesus Christ appeared to him on a Korean mountainside. Christ informed him that he, Moon, was to accomplish a great work, for he was to complete the restoration of mankind started by Jesus himself nearly two thousand years earlier. In this way, Christianity was to be reborn. In its new, Moon-mediated form, it would embrace people of all the Christian denominations.

According to Moon's own story, this experience led him to devote himself to intensive Bible study and long hours of prayer. He claims that he was also given many subsequent visions spanning many years, in the course of which he was allowed to converse directly with Old Testament characters such as Abraham, Isaac, Jacob, Moses and Elijah, New Testament personalities like Peter, Paul and John the Baptist, figures from more recent church history such as Wesley, and founders of other world religions including Muhammad, Confucius and the Buddha. Moon maintains that he is able to move freely in the spirit realm and is the medium through which divine revelations reach people living today. Such experiences have helped reinforce Moon's developing beliefs and to strengthen his conviction that he is God's special envoy to this disunited twentieth-century world with its competing Christian churches.

During the Second World War Sun Myung Moon studied electrical engineering at Waseda University, Tokyo, though it is not clear whether he ever graduated or went on to use his studies to earn a living. Subsequently, however, he became a very successful businessman and still carries on his interests in industries such as pharmaceutics, tuna fish, ginseng tea and air rifles, alongside his religious activities. Before prosperity came to him, however, further revelations in 1945 convinced him that he was the absolute victor of heaven and earth. It was then that he adopted his present name, which means 'Shining sun and moon', and founded the Broad Sea Church in Korea. He seems to have been closely associated with an extreme branch of Pentecostalism which believed that Korea was to be the site of the New Jerusalem and the birthplace of a new Messiah. His own Presbyterian Church excommunicated him in 1948 because of his unorthodox beliefs and activities.

Meanwhile, in 1946 Moon had been imprisoned by the communists. His followers describe this as a period of bitter persecution on account of his religious beliefs, and he is said to have endured this ordeal with great courage, providing a shining example to other fellow sufferers. 'In the bitterness of the concentration camp his selfless giving brought admiration, friendship and a lasting respect from other prisoners', says one of the sect's handouts. He was released by the advancing United States forces in 1950. Five years later he was back in prison, accused of draft-dodging and immorality, but he was soon set free when the prosecution failed to prove its case.

In 1954 Moon founded the Holy Spirit Association for the Unification of World Christianity, now known more usually as the Unification Church but also using a variety of other titles such as the One World Crusade and the New Hope Crusade. With the spread of his church, which is closely aligned with extremely right-wing politics, has gone the growth of Moon's business enterprises. He himself is believed to be worth many millions of pounds and his church does not appear to be short of money.

The year 1957 saw the publication of the first edition of *Divine Principle*, a book written by a close associate, giving Moon's beliefs in great detail and first written in Korean. Subsequent editions have appeared in English.

Another very significant event in his church's history occurred in 1960 when Moon married Hak-Ja Han. A previous marriage had broken up in 1954 because, so Moon explains, his first wife could neither understand nor accept his religion. There is some dispute as to whether Hak-Ja Han is Moon's second or fourth wife. What is not in doubt is that they claim to be the True Parents whom Moonies are expected to call Father and Mother, who have produced eight children of their own, but who are believed to have established a far greater family, the Divine Family consisting of all those who have embraced Moon's teaching.

In response to another of his many divine visions, Moon moved from Korea in 1972 and settled in a mansion on an Irvington, New York, estate. Some of his critics make much of the fact that this house cost him $700,000, but Anglicans who try to use this argument are quickly reminded by the Moonies of the Church Commissioners' millions! In 1975 Moon began his world-wide mission proper by despatching three missionaries to each of ninety-five countries.

Sun Myung Moon and his followers believe that the 1980s will mark the time of the revelation of the Messiah, who will perfect the work begun but not completed by Jesus. The implication of the sect's pronouncements is that this Messiah will turn out to be none other than Sun Myung Moon himself. Moonies point out that Moon has never actually made this claim, but every one of his disciples whom I have met, when challenged, has admitted that he believes Sun Myung Moon to be the Messiah.

The Unification Church's beliefs

Most of the sects on the perimeter of Christianity fall into one of two categories. The first contains those which, like

55

Jehovah's Witnesses and Christadelphians, claim to base their teaching entirely upon the Bible. The second category contains those sects which claim an additional divine revelation which either provides the only legitimate interpretation of the Bible (as with Christian Scientists and their book *Science and Health with Key to the Scriptures*), or which provides further revelation to supplement and even to amend the partial and therefore inadequate truths of the biblical revelation (as with Mormons and their additional scriptures, *The Book of Mormon, Doctrine and Covenants* and *Pearl of Great Price*). Along with Mormons and Christian Scientists, the Moonies belong in this second category, for, as we have seen, Sun Myung Moon is reputed to move freely in the spirit world and to experience frequent visions mediating God's truth to twentieth-century man.

Moon's additional truth appears to come largely through clairvoyant and spiritualistic experiences, of which the most important was that initial vision in which, so Moon claims, Jesus showed him that he had been selected to accomplish a great mission and to complete the work Jesus himself began but failed to fulfil. Therefore, in answer to the question 'With what authority do you teach what you do?', Moon replies, 'I spoke with Jesus Christ in the spirit world. And I spoke also with John the Baptist. This is my authority.'[1] So his followers claim, 'With the fullness of time, God has sent His messenger to resolve the fundamental questions of life and the universe. His name is Sun Myung Moon.'[2] Moon, therefore, is believed to herald a Golden Age for man, for after all he himself has asserted, 'He (God) is living in me and I am in the incarnation of him.'[3] It is hardly surprising to find him telling his followers, therefore, 'I am a thinker; I am your brain.'[4]

All of this fits in well with other extravagant claims made about Moon within the Unification Church. He is described as 'absolute victor of heaven and earth' and the spirit world

---

[1] In a speech at New Orleans, Louisiana, 28 October 1973.
[2] *Divine Principle* (The Holy Spirit Association for the Unification of World Christianity, 1973), p. 36.
[3] *New Hope*, p. 36.   [4] *Master Speaks*, 17 May 1973.

is said to have 'bowed down to him' and duly acknowledged him as 'Lord of creation', for he has fought against and triumphed over satanic forces.[5] To the Moonies, therefore, their leader has become a cult figure. He is 'like the physical representation of God. You pray to God, but you pray through our True Parents, Sun Myung Moon and his wife our Mother in the same way that Christians pray through Jesus.'[6]

In the light of such claims, it is not surprising to find that all that is distinctive about the Unification Church's beliefs stems directly from Moon himself. To his followers, Moon speaks for God. He represents divine authority. It is with some justification, therefore, that his followers are described as Moonies. Moreover, it is a title to which they do not object.

This does not mean that the Unification Church neglects the Bible. On the contrary, its members frequently quote the Bible at length and claim that their beliefs are based upon it. The Unification Church's most important publication, *Divine Principle*, is said to be the authoritative interpretation of the Bible. Moon himself has argued strongly for the need of such an interpretation. The Bible is a book of mystery. It does not use plain language. Why, then, asks Moon, has God presented the Bible in symbols and parables if it contains his message to the world? To Moon the answer is simple. God has had to deal with a world of evil where his champions were always in the minority.

If God revealed His strategy too openly or plainly, that information would be used by the enemy against His own champions. That is why the Bible is written as a coded message, so that only God's agents or champions could decipher it – not the enemy.[7]

It does not take much ingenuity to see where Moon is

[5] *Divine Principle*, p. 16.
[6] Rosalind Mitchell, 'Farewell to the Cults' in *Crusade*, January 1978.
[7] Sun Myung Moon. *The New Future of Christianity* (The Holy Spirit Association for the Unification of World Christianity, 1974), pp. 83f.

leading us. 'If you attempt to interpret the Bible literally, word for word, letter for letter, without understanding the nature of the coded message of the Bible, you are liable to make a great mistake.'[8] However, help is at hand. Moon asserts, 'God has called me as His instrument to reveal His message for His present-day dispensation, so that there may be a people prepared for the day of the Lord.'[9] It is against this background that Moon proceeds to set out his own doctrines which, as we shall see, are at variance with the plain teaching of the Bible.

In practical terms, therefore, whatever lip-service is paid to the Bible within the Unification Church, the Bible's authority comes second to that of Sun Myung Moon. Without him to interpret its true meaning, it is less than adequate as a guide to God's truth for modern man. Indeed, those to whom the Bible was first addressed were people whose spiritual and intellectual standard was low, compared with that of today. Now intelligent modern man can understand the Scriptures because in Moon's interpretation all the problems of religion and science are resolved.

Elsewhere, Moon comes clean and admits that his Church's use of the Christian Bible is nothing but a strategic device to help forward the work of proselytizing.

> Until our mission with the Christian Church is over, we must quote the Bible and use it to explain the Divine Principle. After we receive the inheritance of the Christian Church, we shall be free to teach without the Bible.[10]

It becomes clear, then, that far from being biblical in its beliefs, the Unification Church is based entirely on the 'revelations' claimed by Moon. As with other sects, the Bible is then used to support beliefs and practices accepted on extra-biblical grounds.

Because the beliefs of the Unification Church are thus derived from Moon, it is not to be wondered at that those beliefs differ radically from those of a Bible-based Christianity. That will become clear as we proceed.

[8] *Ibid.*, p. 86.   [9] *Ibid.*   [10] *Master Speaks*, March/April 1965, p. 1.

God

The concept of salvation within the Unification Church revolves around the basic idea that God's will has always been to establish one perfect family throughout the world. God himself is believed to be the perfect Father. But a family also needs a Mother. In Sun Myung Moon's theology this position is filled by the Holy Spirit. 'Thus the Holy Spirit is a female spirit, consoling and moving the hearts of the people.'[11] 'There must be a True Mother with a True Father, in order to give rebirth to fallen children as children of goodness. She is the Holy Spirit.'[12] Later we shall see that the essential deity of Jesus Christ is rejected by the Moonies. It follows, therefore, that there is no place within the Unification Church for the orthodox Christian view of God as Trinity.

The first Adam

When God created Adam and Eve and placed them in the garden of Eden, Moon teaches, it was his intention that they should marry, have normal sexual relations and as True Parents establish a perfect family on earth. The divine plan was frustrated by Eve, however, for she allowed herself to be seduced by Satan. Through sexual intercourse with him she was herself infected by evil and then passed that infection to Adam through intercourse with him. Thus Moon and his followers account for the presence of evil in the world.

For reasons that will become apparent later, it is important to notice that Moon interprets the fall in two parts, spiritual and physical. 'Since God created man in spirit and flesh,' it is asserted, 'the fall also took place in spirit and flesh. The fall through the blood relationship between the angel and Eve was the spiritual fall, while that through the blood relationship between Eve and Adam was the physical fall.' Attempting to answer the obvious question of how Eve, a physical being, could be sexually seduced by Satan, a fallen angelic being, the author of *Divine Principle* explains that feelings and sensations 'are felt and responded

[11] *Divine Principle*, p. 215.   [12] *Ibid.*

to in the invisible, or spirit world. Contact between a spirit and an earthly man (who has a spirit) is not very different from contact between two earthly human beings. Therefore, sexual union between a human being and an angel is actually possible.'[13] But precisely what are we being asked to believe? Christians will readily agree that spiritual seduction by Satan is a distinct possibility for any human being, for to that both human experience and the teaching of the Bible clearly testify. To argue, however, as Moon and his followers argue, that a disembodied spirit can engage in physical intercourse with a human female, defies all reason and takes us back into the fantasy world of pagan mythology. Leaving that debate on one side, however, it is clear that in Moonite theology there is a very close link between sin and sexual relations. Perhaps this explains in part why the marriages of Moonies are arranged by their leaders and why long periods of sexual abstinence follow marriage ceremonies.

The second Adam

No-one can doubt that two of the most vital themes in Christian theology are the Person and work of Jesus Christ. Regarding Christ's Person, historic Christianity has always maintained both the deity and the humanity of the Lord. So, for example, one of the creeds affirms that Jesus Christ is 'the only Son of God, eternally begotten of the Father, God from God, Light from Light, true God from true God, begotten not made, one in being with the Father' and later adds, 'He was born of the Virgin Mary, and became man.'[14] Similarly, though theories about the atonement have abounded in the Christian church down through the centuries, mainstream Christianity has always been clear that 'for our salvation, God the Son became man and died for our sins; that he was raised victorious over death and was exalted to the throne of God as our advocate and intercessor; and that he will come as our judge and saviour.'[15] It will be instructive, therefore, to compare and contrast what

[13] *Ibid.*, p. 77. [14] Nicene Creed (Series 3).
[15] The Revised Catechism.

the Unification Church teaches about the Person and work of Christ.

In the first place, Moon and his followers categorically deny the essential deity of Christ. 'Jesus is a man in whom God is incarnate. But he is not God himself,' says the writer of the sect's authoritative exposition of doctrine.[16] Again, 'Jesus attained deity, as a man who fulfilled the purpose of creation, but can by no means be considered God himself.'[17] What this clearly means is that, though they use the language of incarnation, the Moonies deny the very meaning of incarnation and embrace instead the ancient heresy of adoptionism.

When we turn to the work of Christ, we find the Unification Church's view just as unsatisfactory. Moon and his followers believe that, as second Adam, Jesus was sent to accomplish that which the first Adam failed to accomplish, namely the raising up of a perfect humanity through marriage and procreation. In other words, the Second Adam was expected to marry a second Eve and produce a race of sinless children. If this had happened, they assert, Jesus and his wife would have become the True Parents.[18] Then, by his example and that of his wife and children, other perfect families would have been formed and thus God's great family would have spread throughout the world. Once again, however, God's purpose remained unfulfilled, for before Jesus could marry he was crucified. Therefore, his mission failed.[19]

One very noteworthy omission from the Moonies' outline of the purpose of Christ's work is any emphasis upon the cross. This is not accidental, for, according to one of the sect's writers, Christ's death on the cross was not part of God's plan for redemption.[20] Another publication maintains, 'Redemption through the cross cannot completely

[16] *Divine Principle*, p. 13.
[17] Young Oon Kim, *The Divine Principle and Its Application*, pp. 290f. (*New Hope*, *Master Speaks*, *The Divine Principle and Its Application*, and *New Tomorrow* are all published by the Holy Spirit Association for the Unification of World Christianity.)
[18] *Divine Principle*, p. 28.   [19] *Ibid.*, p. 510.
[20] *The Divine Principle and its Application*, pp. 142f.

liquidate our original sin . . . it leaves man's original nature not yet perfectly restored.'[21] The same writer adds that the cross has not been able 'to establish the Kingdom of Heaven on earth', so 'we . . . must realize that Jesus did not come to die on the cross'.[22] It seems, therefore, that for all their leader's alleged visionary encounters with divines such as Wesley, the Moonies have never learnt the truth expressed in the Wesleyan hymn,

> O thou, before the world began
> Ordained a Sacrifice for man,
> And by the eternal Spirit made
> An offering in the sinner's stead;
> Our everlasting Priest art thou,
> Pleading thy Death for sinners now.

If this Christian view of atonement is rejected, what is left in its place? What precisely did Jesus achieve by his death and resurrection? According to the Unification Church, Christ has achieved just spiritual salvation. Full salvation, however, is both spiritual and physical. By putting one's trust in Jesus Christ, therefore, one is only partly saved, claim the Moonies. Again their major theological work makes their position clear. 'If Jesus had not been crucified . . . He would have accomplished the providence of salvation both spiritually and physically. He would have established the Kingdom of Heaven on earth.'[23] But Jesus was crucified and so his mission failed. It follows that 'however devout a man of faith may be, he cannot fulfil physical salvation of redemption through Jesus' crucifixion alone' (for) 'salvation through redemption by the cross is spiritual only'.[24]

The Moonies believe that Jesus was raised spiritually, that is as a spirit man, and because of that fact, although he cannot redeem us physically, he is able to redeem us spiritually. For full salvation, physical as well as spiritual, another divine initiative is needed. They believe that this

---

[21] *Divine Principle*, p. 142. [22] *Ibid.*, p. 143.
[23] *Ibid.*, p. 147. [24] *Ibid.*, p. 148.

divine initiative is to be seen in the emergence of the Lord of the Second Advent.

The Lord of the Second Advent

Unification Church publications do not make clear who this Lord of the Second Advent will be. Some passages suggest that it will be Jesus Christ himself. Others seem to imply the emergence of another figure. There is also some confusion within the Church's membership as to whether the Christ who returns will prove to be Sun Myung Moon himself. Something of this confusion is seen when we compare passages such as the following.

Because God's plan for full human redemption was not fulfilled by Jesus, 'after 2000 years he is returning to earth as a man to complete in full the mission he only partially accomplished. The Kingdom of Heaven on earth will be established at that time . . . (then) . . . the ideal of God is to restore the first God-centred family on earth. With this one model as a centre, all the rest of mankind can be adopted into this family.'[25] It seems clear in this passage that what is in Moon's mind (for he is its author) is the Second Advent of Jesus Christ in person. In similar vein we read elsewhere.

Christ must come again on the earth to accomplish the purpose of the providence of the physical, as well as the spiritual, salvation, by redeeming the original sin which has not been liquidated even through the cross.[26]

On the other hand, there are passages which leave it much more open, with the possibility of interpreting them as pointing to a distinction between Jesus Christ, the Second Adam, and a new Messiah, the Lord of the Second Advent. 'I am telling you,' asserts Moon, 'the Lord of the Second Advent will in fact appear as a son of man with flesh and bones.'[27] The possibility of making such a dis-

[25] *New Tomorrow*, April 1978, p. 21.
[26] *Divine Principle*, p. 148.
[27] *New Tomorrow*, April 1978, p. 21.

tinction between Christ and the Lord of the Second Advent becomes clearer a little later when Moon writes,

> Just as Jesus revealed himself with the new truth, the Lord of the Second Advent will reveal himself with God's new truth for our own time . . . God must send a new ancestor for humanity, to begin a new history.[28]

Then when we turn to *Divine Principle*, what in other places appears only to be implicit, there seems to become explicit. Another Messiah is needed who will be born on earth as King of kings.[29] He will not come in the clouds, as many Christians have always mistakenly believed, for such a view would prove unacceptable to intelligent modern man.[30] Instead, he will be born on earth in the flesh.[31] That being so, 'it is an undeniable fact that the Christ must come again in the flesh, just as in the first coming'.[32] Moreover, the actual location where the Lord of the Second Advent will appear is stated to be Korea.[33]

Reading some of these last passages, especially against the background of the homage closely approaching worship given to Sun Myung Moon within the Unification Church, it is hard to escape the conclusion that his followers are encouraged to believe that he himself, born in Korea in 1920, is in fact the Lord of the Second Advent, the twentieth-century manifestation of the Christ. That this conclusion is legitimate is further substantiated when one reads from Moon's authoritative interpreter,

> the marriage of the lamb prophesied in the 19th chapter of Revelation took place in 1960 . . . Thus the Lord of the Second Advent and His Bride became the True Parents of mankind.[34]

As was pointed out earlier, Sun Myung Moon married his present wife, Hak-Ja Han, in that year. It is not sur-

---

[28] *Ibid.*, p. 22.   [29] *Divine Principle*, p. 510.   [30] *Ibid.*, p. 500.
[31] *Ibid.*   [32] *Ibid.*, p. 510.   [33] *Ibid.*, p. 520.
[34] *The Divine Principle and its Application*, p. 196.

prising, therefore, that although Moon himself has never specifically made the claim that he is the Lord of the Second Advent, I have yet to meet one of his followers who believes him to be anything less.

The Unification Church's methods

The Unification Church operates under various names, runs the One World Crusade, sponsors a number of international cultural and religion-and-science conferences, and encourages its members to engage in community service such as baby-sitting, children's playgroups, and digging the gardens of old people. The main purpose of all these activities is always the same – to make more Moonies and so to add to the Perfect Family.

In their more direct missionary work, Moonies, in common with most of the sects examined in this book and its predecessor,[35] do not wait for potential converts to approach them but are zealous in evangelistic activities. The first contact may be on a street corner, in a shopping centre, at a railway station, or in some other similar public place.

The contact, who is always greeted with a disarming smile, may be invited to contribute to 'Christian missionary work', or to purchase some cheap object, or to take one of the sect's publications such as *New Tomorrow*. At this stage, the missionary will not be anxious to reveal his true identity or to point out the specific beliefs he holds as a follower of Sun Myung Moon. He wishes simply to make a good impression by the friendliness of his approach. So, avoiding any arguments about belief, he will try to agree with almost any point of view expressed by his contact. This is all part of the Unification Church's missionary strategy and is known within the sect as 'heavenly deception'. Although I have found Moonies reluctant to explain what they mean by 'heavenly deception', in practice it seems to mean that sect members may indulge in deliberate deceit for the good of the cause. Thus, using this ploy, Moonies often pass

[35] Maurice C. Burrell and J. Stafford Wright, *Some Modern Faiths* (IVP, 1973).

themselves off as mainstream Christians, and have been known to tell contacts that they have been sent to them by the local vicar or minister and even to claim the support of the diocesan bishop. It is another twentieth-century variant of the old maxim that the means are justified by the end.

If the contact shows more than polite interest, he may be invited to a meal with the local Moonies, or to a meeting, or to a three-day houseparty. Whatever form this follow-up takes, one thing is certain: the potential convert will be subjected to a non-stop verbal onslaught calculated to wear down his resistance and to persuade him to accept the doctrines and, in particular, the authority of Sun Myung Moon. If he is prepared to make such a commitment, the novice is then almost certain to make a clean break with his unbelieving family, to work unceasingly for the Unification Church, and eventually to hand over his money and possessions for the good of the cause. It is by no means uncommon for rich people to become Moonies and to hand over their property to the sect, the squire of Stanton Fitzwarren near Swindon being a recent British example.

Because it plays such an important and decisive part in the Unification Church's proselytizing activities, it is necessary to look carefully at what happens at the local Unification Church centres, where groups of Moonies live together as a community and to which other interested contacts are invited from time to time. Fortunately, this is a well-documented area, with valuable evidence from former members of the sect and from others who left after initial interest before becoming fully committed.

A one-time agnostic who is now an Anglican ordinand, whom we shall call Peter, travelling with a friend in New Zealand, found himself becoming involved almost by accident. The two friends were looking for somewhere to stay in Wellington when they were approached by a young man they came to know as William, who said he was a representative of a Christian organization which could offer them hospitality. The two friends went along with William to a large house, with one very large communal room and many smaller rooms, which housed some twenty-five residents. Peter and his companion soon discovered that they had unsuspectingly walked into a Unification Church community, one of thousands of such places scattered throughout the world.

William was given the task of staying with the two friends at all times. He subjected them to a continuous verbal barrage about Sun Myung Moon and the Unification Church, but never left them together to discuss with each other what they were being told. When in an attempt to choke William off they began treating his onslaught lightheartedly, he responded by contriving to separate them from each other. Peter claims that they were then indoctrinated separately for periods of up to two hours a time.

When the two friends decided that enough was enough and that they must leave, the whole community of Moonies gathered in the hall by the main door, accompanied by a large Alsatian dog, and William and a German woman who appeared to be in a position of authority in the community angrily accused them of living off the community and giving nothing in return. After such exchanges they were challenged to turn their backs on their parents, to give up everything and to join the Unification Church. Eventually they managed to leave on friendlier terms by explaining that they had to return to England but that they would follow up the teachings of Sun Myung Moon there.

Peter sincerely believes that had he been alone in that Unification Church house, without the moral support of his friend, he might not have found the strength to leave. He claims that the psychological pressures to stay were intense. His companion feels the same way.

The following extract from the *Reader's Digest* of June 1977 describes techniques sometimes used by the Moonies.

The Moonies convert recruits into cultists by programming every minute of their waking hours. Hardcore Moonies are assigned to all novices, talking to them incessantly, never giving them a chance to talk or ask questions. Underfed and with only four or five hours' sleep a night, these youngsters are psychologically worn down until they're brought under complete mind control and fall into a trance, somewhat like an auto-hypnotic state where their wills aren't their own – they belong to Moon.

Dr Charles Edwards, who wrote the article, writes from the heart, for his son became deeply involved with the sect and was released only after many traumatic experiences for himself and his parents. With the passage of time, some Moonies do become more sophisticated and subtle in their approach. There is more than enough evidence to suggest, however, that the more aggressive approach is still widespread enough to make it disturbing to a generation familiar with intensive indoctrination techniques.

Young people between 18 and 25, especially students, appear to be among the most susceptible to the Unification Church's approaches. There have been a number of instances of promising undergraduates and post-graduate research students who have forsaken their courses or prospects of a rewarding career to become Moonies. In a letter to the editor of *The Times* on 1 March 1980, David Vaughan described an all-too-familiar sequence of events.

I have just returned from California after a fruitless mission to recover my 23-year-old son. He is with the Unification Church whose cult leader is a Mr Moon. Francis flew to San Francisco on November 1 for two weeks holiday. He is the only British graduate in energy technology at both bachelor and masters level. I was able to see him on only two short occasions of a nine day visit and then on their property and never alone. His college tutor then flew out to help me and was granted just one visit on similar terms. There is no question that due to their well-documented teachings and harsh living conditions, the balance of his mind has been disturbed. United States immigration officials seem powerless to help even though he is classed as an overstay, his visitor's visa having expired three months ago. He is required to work up to sixteen hours a day rug cleaning, laundering, sorting reject fruit and vegetables, flower selling, preparing meals and enrolling new recruits.

Conversion to the sect is often accompanied by complete alienation from family and friends, as many case histories prove. Even the Moonies have become alarmed about the bad publicity this has brought them, and now arrange conferences at which parents can learn more about the religion which their children have embraced. Long before that, however, a group of people in Britain, including parents of Moonies and former members of the sect, formed an organization called FAIR (Family Action Information and Rescue) to help the worried parents of sect members to free their children from the Unification Church.

The Unification Church and Christianity

The points of fundamental disagreement between the followers of Sun Myung Moon and the disciples of Jesus Christ must now be obvious to all who have read the foregoing pages. They concern both doctrine and practice. In particular, however, it is necessary to draw attention to five areas of conflict.

First, there is the basic conflict about authority. Whereas adherents of the Unification Church believe that their leader is the channel through whom new, extra-biblical truths are conveyed from God to them, mainstream Christians believe that the truth of God, revealed fully and finally in Jesus Christ, is contained in the Bible. We look for the incarnate Word in the written Word. The test of any religion, therefore, is not whether its leader happens to believe that he has a message from God, or whether he is then able to persuade others to accept his views, but whether the message he proclaims is faithful to the teaching of the Bible. Christians believe that much of what Moon and his followers believe and practise is found wanting when measured against the yardstick of Scripture.

Secondly, because they wish to remain faithful to the biblical revelation, Christians must view with considerable concern the rejection of the doctrine of the Trinity which stems from Moon's view of the 'female' and 'mother' Holy Spirit working with God the Father to produce the perfect family. For reasons stated earlier, the historic belief in God as Father, Son and Holy Spirit has to be retained if the Bible's authority is respected.

Thirdly, Christians faithful to Christ as Lord have no option but to reject the exalted position given to Sun Myung Moon within the Unification Church. For them, the gospel is the good news that God in Christ was reconciling the world to himself. And 'God in Christ' means God in the same historical Jesus Christ who came, lived, died, rose, ascended, and is coming again. To set up someone as 'another Christ' is an act of apostasy that Christians have always opposed from the days of Paul onwards. The choice, therefore, is clear. We cannot serve Jesus Christ and Sun Myung Moon, for loyalty to the one means the inevitable rejection of the other.

Fourthly, because of their beliefs about the relationship between God and man, Christians must reject the proselytizing techniques employed by the Unification Church. Christians believe that God created man in such a way that man is free to respond in love and service to God and, also, that man is free to refuse to love and serve him. They recall that Jesus never forced himself or his teaching upon people but left people free to decide for themselves. Therefore, as his followers, they cannot be anything but appalled at the intensive techniques used by the Unification Church as they attempt to win converts. To submit potential recruits to the kind of methods described earlier is not Christian evangelism. Such methods ought never to be used in the advancement of a system of belief. They are the more hateful when they are said to be employed in the name of the Christ who came to set people free.

Finally, it follows that anyone who has understood the gospel of Christ must regard as blasphemous a view which states that the mission of Jesus failed, that the cross was an unmitigated disaster, that the salvation offered to us in Jesus is inadequate, and that we need another Messiah to provide us with full salvation. The New Testament, in contrast, makes it clear that all that is necessary for full salvation has already been done by Christ.[36]

[36] For further reading see John Allan, *The Rising of the Moon* (IVP, 1980).

Summary of main differences

Unification Church   *Christianity*

Authority

Moon's interpretations of the Bible and his extra-biblical statements are regarded as God-given truths.

As the Word of God, the Bible is the yardstick against which all claims to truth (including those of Moon) have to be measured.

God

The world's True Parents are God himself as Father and the Holy Spirit as Mother.

God is Trinity, Father, Son and Holy Spirit, three Persons within the unity of the Godhead.

Jesus

Though not God in the full sense, as the Second Adam raised up by God his mission was to save mankind by forming the Perfect Family. That mission failed because he died on the cross before he was able to complete it. God therefore raised up another Saviour, the Lord of the Second Advent (Sun Myung Moon) to do what Jesus failed to achieve.

As the one who is both God and Man, Jesus was sent by his Father to reveal God to us and to die on the cross to save us. By his death and the vindication of his resurrection, Jesus has done all that is necessary for mankind's full salvation.

Salvation

This is obtained when human beings allow themselves to become

By appropriating by faith all that Christ has done on mankind's behalf, we

71

adopted members of Sun Myung Moon's family by becoming his disciples.

are saved from sin and given new life in Christ. 'There is no salvation in anyone else at all, for there is no other name under heaven granted to men, by which we may receive salvation' (Acts 4:12).

Church

Though claiming to be a movement for the unification of world-wide Christianity, it denies much of what mainstream Christianity affirms. It has set up another rival church in opposition to the historic Christian church.

The one true church consists of all who through faith have received Jesus as Saviour and who acknowledge him as Lord.

Family

Because of the belief that Sun Myung Moon's family is the true Church, all other natural family ties take second place and are often broken completely.

'Honour your father and your mother.'

5. The Divine Light Mission

'I will give you salvation, if you surrender your lives to me.' This is the unequivocal claim of Guru Maharaj Ji, leader of the Divine Light Mission. Born in Hardwar, India, on 10 December 1957, the young Guru is now well known in many parts of Britain, Europe and North America. He and his followers, said to number more than six million, claim that Guru Maharaj Ji is to people today what Jesus was to people two thousand years ago, an incarnation of the divine. Therefore his disciples believe in him and so worship, adore and obey him.

But who is he and what are his claims? And how does his teaching compare with or differ from that of the mainstream Christian churches? What methods do he and his followers use to spread his teaching and to win converts? How should Christians react to the Divine Light Mission? These are some of the questions this chapter seeks to answer.

The Divine Light Mission's guru

The Mission was founded in 1949 by Shri Maharaj Ji, the present Guru's Hindu father. According to one of the Mission's publications,

> While the world's scientists were busy inventing the atom bomb, the greatest scientist, the Saviour of the Universe ... came down from the Himalayas ... and started giving the antidote to nuclear warfare and ma-

terial craziness. Whoever went to him and followed him became a dedicated disciple attaining everlasting peace.[1]

As numbers began to increase, Shri Maharaj Ji founded the Divine Light Mission. Its members claim that ever since its inception the Mission has 'dedicated itself to propagating the tenets of universal love and brotherhood of men. Above all, the Mission has spread the knowledge of peace to millions of men and women all over the world.'[2]

When his father died in August 1966, Guru Maharaj Ji, though only eight years old and the youngest son, succeeded him. At that time he was attending a Roman Catholic mission school in India. A Divine Light Mission leaflet paints a colourful picture of the accession.

When thousands were weeping, Guru Maharaj Ji stepped forward and said, 'Dear children of God, why are you weeping? Haven't you learned the lesson that your Master taught you? The Perfect Master never dies. Maharaj Ji is here, amongst you now. Recognize Him, obey Him, and adore Him!'

The young boy was apparently accepted on those terms and quickly won over the support of his dead father's disciples and, more importantly, the loyalty of the rest of his family. By 1969 he was claiming thousands of converts at his ashram on the banks of the Ganges. That same year he despatched his first missionaries to England. In November 1970 a rally of 1½ million people listened to him at India Gate, New Delhi, after he had ridden through the city in a gold chariot surrounded by elephants, camels, and his devotees. Two years later Divine Light Mission centres had been established in many of the world's leading cities. An American headquarters was set up in Denver, Colorado, whilst here in Britain his portly figure could be seen on posters all over the country. Though the publicity seemed to die down for a year or two (probably because of a bitter dispute within his family about his behaviour), his disciples

---

[1] Record jacket of *Thine to Thee*.   [2] *Ibid.*

are once again actively engaged in their attempts to convert the world to their Perfect Master and are presently engaged in a renewed recruitment drive in Britain.

Guru Maharaj Ji's followers describe 'Him' (they always use the capital letter as a mark of respect) as 'the Satguru, the True Revealer of Light and Remover of darkness, the Perfect one, destined in fulfilment of all prophecies to enlighten the world'. Others are less flattering in their evaluation. A fellow Indian has called him a typical Asian phoney. A journalist said he was a gross, 'Westernized Hindu with a penchant for Rolls Royces and clumsy parables'.[3]

In 1974 the Guru caused a stir by marrying a former American airline stewardess, and now has two young children. Soon after his marriage rifts began appearing within the movement and some of his relatives have accused him of haunting night-clubs, drinking, dancing, and eating meat, activities from which he demands the abstinence of his followers. His mother, Mataji, denounced him, said that he was no longer the leader of the Divine Light Mission, and claimed that his place has been taken by his eldest brother, Bal Bhagwan Ji. At the time of writing, the dispute continues, though it seems to have had no marked effect among the majority of the Guru's devotees and his press officer has claimed that it has all been exaggerated by the press. Nevertheless, it is obvious that all is not well among the Guru's relatives, and William Petersen has commented, 'Who knows what the future holds for Guru Maharaj Ji? A few years ago they were heralding the Millennium, but now the Holy Family itself is engaged in a Holy War.'[4]

Despite such friction within the sect, its influence has spread to many parts of the world, with large numbers of devotees in Europe and America. It has made its greatest impact upon the young, especially the 18–25 age group, and claims a considerable following among students.

It appears that the Guru's followers have reacted against the excessive materialism of the twentieth-century western

[3] Bart Milner, *The Times*, 29 September 1973.
[4] William Petersen, *Those Curious New Cults*, p. 246.

world. They like to live together in their small, religious communities, which they call ashrams.

Since the Mission's initial impact upon Britain in 1973, when the Guru Puja at Alexandra Palace, held between 13 and 15 July, attracted 4,000 people, its membership has grown steadily if unspectacularly. A series of gatherings at Olympia in London during August 1980, at which Guru Maharaj Ji himself addressed his followers, attracted several thousand people. There may now be about 1,000 British devotees of the Guru. Only time will show whether the Divine Light Mission will become what Bryan Wilson, the Oxford sociologist, calls an established sect, or whether, like so many of its predecessors, it will disappear from history almost as suddenly as it arose.

The Divine Light Mission's beliefs

As we shall see later, the Guru offers an experience rather than a creed. One radio commentator[5] went so far as to assert that the Divine Light Mission 'has no doctrinal teachings'. That is far from the truth. Although much emphasis is placed on experience, that experience (the knowledge of God which the Guru claims to be able to impart to his followers) has to be understood in the light of a definite doctrinal framework within which the Guru operates.

Although this framework includes elements of Sikhism and Christianity, and indeed other world religions, the religion of Guru Maharaj Ji stems largely from the Hinduism within which he was nurtured. In particular, the Guru seems to have derived many of his ideas from the *Upanishads*, a collection of Hindu sacred writings which originated between 800 and 300 BC, which speculate about Ultimate Reality, and which put forward a view of God that is very close to pantheism, the belief that God is all and that all is God. Guru Maharaj Ji has tried to popularize this idea and has produced a way of instant salvation through the reception of 'knowledge'. This will become

[5] William Nicholson in the BBC programme 'The Lobster Pot', autumn 1978.

clearer as we begin to look at such crucial areas of belief as those concerned with God, salvation, the Guru, and Scripture.

God

Divine Light Mission publications describe God as 'Cosmic Energy' and say that God exists in light which is without cause, the natural state of such Cosmic Energy. God has always existed in this form and always will so exist. 'This Cosmic Energy is so subtle that we cannot comprehend it with our minds because the human mind is very gross in comparison.'[6] They point out that whereas Cosmic Energy is infinite, we are finite. 'The Mind, however, does have the capacity of directly experiencing this Cosmic Energy, and after regular and prolonged contact with it, the mind eventually merges with it; it becomes attuned ... to the Universal Mind.' When this occurs, that is 'when the mind of man is in exact accord with the Universal Mind', man experiences 'bliss, mokshya, liberation, nirvana, salvation, or samadhi'.[7]

Students of Hinduism will not need to be reminded of how closely this accords with ideas in the *Upanishads* where doctrine revolves around two key words, brahman and atman. Brahman stands for ultimate reality, the idea of a world soul or a universal divine principle. Atman stands for the individual self or soul. The ideal, according to the *Upanishads*, is that this individual self (the atman) should be at one with the ultimate reality (the brahman). It should be noted, however, that there is no idea of a personal relationship between 'God' and the individual, but rather the absorption of the individual into Ultimate Reality. His destiny is to become like a drop of water lost in a bucket that is full.

Salvation

Closely related to the ideas set out above is the Hindu doctrine of samsara, belief in the transmigration of the soul

---

[6] *Science and Religion*, a leaflet published by the Divine Light Mission.
[7] *Ibid.*

from one life to another through a cycle of rebirths. While on earth the soul is believed to be caught up in a web of illusion. How is it to escape? Hindus believe that every activity of thought or deed sets in motion a series of inevitable consequences, just as the stone thrown into a pond creates an expanding circle of ripples. Present conduct results in rebirth, to either a higher or a lower form of existence. Release (mokshya), that is salvation from this seemingly endless cycle of birth, death and rebirth, is achieved by breaking evil passions and illusions and by attaining a calm and passionless state. Then the individual, liberated from the illusion that characterizes life, becomes united with, indeed absorbed within, the divine.

Although Guru Maharaj Ji and his followers use different terminology, their views are almost identical. So salvation is not to be interpreted in the traditional Christian sense of being set free from sin and for life, but rather as being set free from the illusions of the world. Then, and only then, can the individual achieve unity with Ultimate Reality or Cosmic Energy. Until this happens, the individual is imprisoned in the endless chain of cause and effect which results in rebirth after rebirth.

What must a person do to be thus liberated? The Divine Light Mission's reply is, 'He must receive Knowledge.' It would be a mistake to think that this Knowledge is merely an intellectual grasp of certain religious propositions, however. Indeed, within this sect there is no call for devotees to use their intellects. On the contrary, it seems to be one of the Guru's basic requirements that his followers do not think, but feel. Knowledge means direct experience of God, that is of Cosmic Energy. In order that he may gain such experience, the potential convert must turn to the only person in any given age in whom this Cosmic Energy is manifested in human form. After that, constant meditation will eventually result in the human mind merging with the Divine Mind.

The Guru
We are now in a position to consider the place that Guru Maharaj Ji occupies at the heart of Divine Light Mission

beliefs. He is not regarded simply as another guru (*i.e.* one spiritual teacher among many) but as Satguru (*i.e.* the Perfect Teacher who is in some sense a human manifestation of the divine). Thus his followers describe him as the one dispenser of that true Knowledge without which the human soul cannot achieve unity with Ultimate Reality. The sect's literature, films, records and speakers leave us in no doubt that the Guru's followers regard him as the avatar of our time, that is, the perfectly God-realized soul.

It is necessary to remind ourselves of the Mission's Hindu origins to understand this phenomenon. Like Hindus generally, the Guru's followers believe that Ultimate Reality, Cosmic Energy, 'God', has revealed himself in a whole series of incarnations or avatars down through the ages. Jesus Christ was one such avatar; Guru Maharaj Ji is another. The Divine Light Mission goes further, maintaining that what Jesus Christ was to people living two thousand years ago Guru Maharaj Ji is to people living today. 'The disciples of Guru Maharaj Ji have always said that like Guru Maharaj Ji, Jesus was the Satguru or God-realized Soul of His time.'[8] They then argue that it is a mistake for people living today to focus their attention simply upon Jesus (a past manifestation). What today's world needs is to be found pre-eminently in the contemporary manifestation of the divine, that is in Guru Maharaj Ji.

There is no doubt, therefore, about what members of the Divine Light Mission believe concerning Guru Maharaj Ji. Their publications reiterate their faith. He is 'the treasure house of unlimited happiness', 'the Giver of Knowledge', 'the storehouse of unlimited peace' and 'the ocean of kindness'. He is able to relieve all the suffering there is on this planet and has promised to do this within his present life-span. His followers believe he has already made a very impressive start.

One devotee told me that his conversion to the Guru had transformed his life. 'Nothing is a problem any more. I have no problems in this life.' A second claimed, 'Guru Maharaj Ji is inside me and He is inside every one of us.'

[8] *The Divine Times*, 26 May 1973, a newspaper published by the DLM.

A third said, 'Guru Maharaj Ji has satisfied every need in me.' Those who have read the sect's literature will have seen similar testimonies. In *The Divine Times*, a fifty-five-year-old Scots woman wrote, 'I want to tell people from the roof tops what Guru Maharaj Ji means in my life. At last my search for God is over. He walks among men.'[9]

Because they regard their Guru as divine, his followers do not hesitate to worship him. When I attended a public meeting organized by the Divine Light Mission, I found at the front of the hall a table decorated with embroidered cloths and colourful flowers. Immediately behind the table, but raised up so that all could see it, was a large photograph of Guru Maharaj Ji. It quickly became evident that this photograph was intended to be the focal point for everything that took place during the two-and-a-half-hour programme of talks, films and songs at this public meeting. As members of the Divine Light Mission entered the hall, they approached the photograph and prostrated themselves before it. I watched a group of devotees who appeared to be in a trance-like state, as with glazed eyes they gazed enraptured at the Guru's likeness. They sang, as Christians might sing of Jesus, 'The way to liberation through You has come', and, 'The Lord of the Universe has come to us this day, He's come to show us the light, the life, the way.' Their songs included the invitation, 'Open your hearts to Him', followed by the response, 'I give myself to You, O Lord; do with me what You will.'

This unquestioning dedication to the young Guru is demonstrated on the jacket of the record *Thine to Thee*, produced, so it claims, 'by the grace of Guru Maharaj Ji'. The singers write:

This record is just a small token of the love that we feel in our hearts for our Lord, Guru Maharaj Ji. For He has shown us such a Light. He has revealed to us such Knowledge, that our searching for Truth has ended, and with it our fears, anxieties and ignorance. . . . We can now do nothing but spend our life and our energy singing

[9] *Ibid.*

the praises of Him who revealed this inner beauty to us
– He whose personality is perfect and radiant Light, our
Lord and Father Guru Maharaj Ji. Before He opened
our hearts, we did not know love at all. Now, by His
Grace, we are able to know true love for God and all
mankind.

It is sometimes said that although the Guru's followers
make extravagant claims for him, he himself is much more
modest. The evidence does not support this view. 'I will
give you salvation if you surrender your lives to me,' he
says. Because he is 'almighty', 'all-powerful', 'the only one
who saves souls from dark and dangerous pitfalls and bless-
es them with new life', he demands obedience as well as
worship and adoration. And all three are given to him by
his followers.

Scripture

Earlier it was pointed out that the beliefs and practices of
the Divine Light Mission have elements of Hinduism and
Sikhism. Until quite recently, the sect's publications used
to quote from Indian and other sacred writings, appearing
to treat them all as equally authoritative. Thus, under the
heading, 'What the Scriptures Say', one copy of *The Divine
Times* stated, 'All Scriptures glorify the Divine Knowledge'.
The reader was invited to send to the editor suitable quotations from any scriptures. This seemed to support the
view that all religions were pursuing the same search for
knowledge. It has always been true, however, that no matter what lip-service was paid to other religions, the Divine
Light Mission has believed itself to be the channel through
which the full Truth has come. Real spiritual knowledge is
given only by the grace of Guru Maharaj Ji and through
the agency of one of his mahatmas. It is not surprising to
find, therefore, that the sect has now given up its practice
of referring to other scriptures and quotes only from the
statements of Guru Maharaj Ji. Indeed, there is a growing
reluctance among its members to value scriptures at all,
even those of Indian religions from which many of the
Divine Light Mission's teachings come. Members wish to

discuss only their own subjective experience and refuse to recognize any yardstick against which that experience is to be judged or evaluated.

The Divine Light Mission's methods

As often within modern alternatives to mainstream Christianity, the Divine Light Mission has a two-tier membership, an élite and the rank-and-file followers. The ordinary, rank-and-file members of the sect are called premies. Some two thousand or more others have been designated by Guru Maharaj Ji as mahatmas (literally 'high-souled') and to them has been given this power to reveal the Knowledge to potential converts.

This 'revelation of Knowledge' has been criticized often as a form of intensive indoctrination.

> When taking 'Knowledge' novices concentrate for several hours on the music of the vibes and chant over and over again that Guru Maharaj Ji is perfect and has been sent by God to reveal his presence. Suddenly the novice is jabbed sharply in the eyes by the Mahatma and sees, so it is said, the Divine Light of God Himself.[10]

The same writer went on to describe how this 'conversion experience' is followed by meditation involving the constant repetition of the divine name (which he called auto-suggestion) and by satsang, 'Divine Light services held every day, where each premie in turn is expected to repeat in every conceivable way that the world is a dark place desperately needing the Light which only the Guru can provide' (which he called group-suggestion). The writer commented that after a few months of this treatment the Mission could probably get its converts to do almost anything.[11]

Testimony from the Guru's converts suggests that the journalist's description of 'taking Knowledge' was not far from the truth. Thus in a BBC programme broadcast in the autumn of 1978 a Divine Light Mission member

[10] Bart Milner, *op. cit.*   [11] *Ibid.*

claimed that the Guru had enabled her to experience God through instant enlightenment and said that she had seen the light after a mahatma had put pressure on her eyeballs. That there is some pressure on the eyes is borne out by similar accounts from other devotees.

I have not seen any denial of this technique by the Divine Light Mission. What they do deny, however, is that it is a form of brainwashing, claiming that 'the Knowledge of Guru Maharaj Ji is of a simple and inner meditation, peacefully bestowed and peacefully practised'.[12] The sect maintains that old ladies, children, housewives and businessmen – ordinary people with no time for the outlandish or esoteric – have received the Knowledge and practise it daily, and that it results in their becoming more peaceful, tolerant and understanding. Interviews with sect members and with the sometimes very anxious relatives of sect members lead me to conclude, however, that the description of their techniques as intensive indoctrination is accurate. Moreover, relatives of the Guru's converts have not found that their own experience of their sons, daughters, husbands, wives, and brothers and sisters supports the view that membership of the Divine Light Mission makes them more peaceful, tolerant and understanding. On the contrary, families have been broken up, businesses have been ruined, and houses have been taken over, all in the name and for the sake of Guru Maharaj Ji. Nor is there much doubt in my mind that the kind of emotional singing and chanting that goes on at the Mission's rallies leads members into a state close to mass hysteria.

Some Divine Light Mission devotees live in spiritual communities called ashrams (literally 'shelters'). The sect's publications describe them as 'places across the world where disciples of the Lord are living and where satsang (spiritual discourse) can be heard'. Ashram dwellers must be celibate and are required also to abstain from alcohol, tobacco and meat. The number of Mission members in Britain is probably less than 10,000, but the sect's numer-

[12] Letter to *The Times* by Glen Whittaker, a leading member, 11 October 1973.

ical weakness is belied by its publicity and its proselytizing zeal, for there can be few towns that have not felt the impact of Guru Maharaj Ji's followers or whose populations have not learnt to recognize the familiar features of the rather portly young Guru from advertisements in their local newspapers.

From the Guru downwards, everything in the sect is divine. Divine Rummage Collectors organize Divine Jumble Sales. There is a Divine Sales International operating throughout those countries where the Mission has its branches. The Guru has spoken of building a Divine City in Nevada and of opening a Divine (fee-paying!) School in London. A copy of the Mission's newspaper, *The Divine Times*, carried an invitation for 'premies who are interested in forming a Divine Dance Theatre' to contact the advertiser.

The Guru's teachings and his claim to give divine enlightenment to those wishing to experience God are spread through public meetings at which spiritual discourse (satsangs) are given, through film shows, records, songs (accompanied by the guitar), *The Divine Times* and other publications, and through personal contact.

The Divine Light Mission and Christianity

As Christians we believe that God's truth has come to us in the unique revelation he has given of himself in the Person of Jesus Christ. He who in former times spoke to our forefathers in fragmentary and varied fashion through the prophets, has in this final age spoken to us in his Son.[13] Believing that we cannot regard it as anything less than blasphemous when another, be he a Guru Maharaj Ji, a Sun Myung Moon, or anyone else, allows his followers to place him on the same level as, or even a higher level than, Christ. We believe that Jesus is *the* way, *the* truth, and *the* life, and that no-one comes to the Father except through him.[14] We shall need to examine the Divine Light Mission's denial of this truth a little later, but obviously it is of

[13] Hebrews 1:1ff.   [14] John 14:6.

paramount significance when considering the relationship between this sect and mainstream Christianity. We need to remind ourselves, however, that our attitude to this and any other religious group (and, indeed, to those professing no religion) should be an attitude of love.

The fact that we are diametrically opposed to much of the Guru's teaching, and to the way in which his followers try to spread it, should not blind us to the transparent sincerity of many of his followers. It would be quite wrong to assume that all Divine Light Mission devotees are wilfully ignorant of the truth as it is in Jesus. It is much nearer the mark to say that many of them are seeking a spiritual satisfaction they have failed to find elsewhere, often in institutional religion. The guilt may be ours rather than theirs.

Nor is anything to be gained from merely poking fun at the young Guru's portly figure or squeaky voice. Such ridicule is not only un-Christian but is inadequate as an answer to error.

We also need to recognize with humility that there are some good emphases within the Divine Light Mission which Christians might profitably emulate. Many of the Guru's disciples have forsaken what they regard as the despicable rat race of a materialistic age for a simpler lifestyle based on spiritual values. They regard the search for truth as of more consequence than status or possessions. Their priority is to be at one with the Infinite. We may well believe that their view of the Infinite is inadequate and their way to harmony is unscriptural, but let us not be uncharitable about their spiritual hunger and their desire for spiritual knowledge. We can surely thank God that they have felt the need to be right with him.

Again, our Christian commitment should not blind us to the sacrificial zeal of many of the Guru's followers. We may think it odd and inconsistent that their leader calls them to follow a path that he himself does not tread. As one critic has said,

The Perfect Master himself is sitting in a half-million dollar estate in the States . . . surrounded by a fleet of cars, Mercedes-Benz, Lotus sports car, motor-cycles, swimming-pool. God can have whatever he wants![15]

He allows himself to be treated with pomp and ceremony and lives in luxury, yet calls upon his followers to deny themselves and follow him. As his own press officer has said, 'Guru Maharaj Ji lives on gifts given to him by his followers. And they want him to live very well.'[16] No matter how his devotees seek to rationalize this basic inconsistency, however, it bears no comparison with Jesus who, himself having little in the way of earthly possessions, invited his followers to *be like him*, and to take up their cross daily and go after him. Having admitted all that, however, there is no doubt that many members of the Divine Light Mission have forsaken all for Guru Maharaj Ji. How many Christians would be ready to go as far in their loyalty to Jesus Christ?

Although we shall wish to treat them with love and with a proper recognition of all that is good in their religion, the fact remains, however, that there is much in what they believe and teach which comes into direct conflict with Christianity. This becomes clear as we look more closely at those four areas of belief already outlined.

God
Christians will readily agree with the Divine Light Mission that God-is both eternal and infinite. The Bible speaks of God's 'eternal power and deity'[17] and certainly reminds us that he is far greater than anything our minds are able to comprehend.[18] We shall not wish to disagree with the Divine Light Mission when they tell us that this infinite God has to reveal himself before we can know him and that man's highest bliss is to be at one with God, for all of this is an integral part of mainstream Christianity.

On other counts, however, Christians will disagree with the sect's view of God. It is necessary to point out that the Divine Light Mission's view does not go far enough, that

[15] Carol Williams in BBC's 'Checkpoint', 30 May 1979.
[16] Joe Anthill, *ibid.*   [17] Romans 1:20, RSV.   [18] Isaiah 40:12ff. *etc.*

it falls short of the biblical view, for Scripture shows us that it is not enough to see God merely in terms of Cosmic Energy existing in uncaused light, interesting though this highly symbolic picture may be. God is not some blind scientific force, operating in an impersonal way. God is holy; God is merciful; God is love.[19] He is the Creator who made us, the Father who sustains us and the Redeemer who saves us.[20] And, according to the Bible, he is much more besides.

Our second complaint is that the Divine Light Mission's view of God is false as well as inadequate. It maintains that God has revealed himself in a whole series of avatars or incarnations, which include Jesus Christ along with other former religious leaders, but of which the contemporary incarnation is Guru Maharaj Ji. We shall need to look more closely at this belief in due course.

Salvation

Although the followers of Guru Maharaj Ji speak in terms of the human mind being brought into harmony with the Divine Mind and also of salvation or liberation, their ideas are far removed from the Christian view of salvation. Christians do not believe that union with God means the merging of the finite human mind with the infinite Divine Mind. Nor do they believe that harmony with God is simply an experience of Cosmic Energy. The mainstream Christian belief is in a God who is personal and in a relationship with him that is essentially a Person-to-person relationship. So God is our Father and we, in Christ, have become his children.[21] Because of the love he has first shown to us in Christ, we love both him and one another.[22]

This is a dimension of religion that is entirely absent from the Guru's teachings. Although his devotees speak much of their love for one another and especially of their love for Guru Maharaj Ji, they do not speak of love for God himself. This is because their view of God is closer to that

[19] Isaiah 6; Luke 6:36; 1 John 4:8.
[20] Genesis 1:26; Matthew 6:26ff.; 2 Corinthians 5:19.
[21] Matthew 6; John 1:12. [22] 1 John 4:7ff.

of the Hindu *Upanishads* than that of the Bible. Christians can love God, because to them he is their heavenly Father, but by no stretch of the imagination can one love God if one believes that he is Cosmic Energy surrounded by un-caused Light.

The clear teaching of the Bible about sin and salvation is very different from the views of the Guru and his follow-ers, and revolves around a number of important facts. God made us for fellowship with himself and intended that fel-lowship to be expressed in love and obedience.[23] By going our own way rather than his, we have created a barrier between God and ourselves, so the Bible describes man as a sinner and a transgressor. In our natural state, all of us (without exception) are out of harmony with God. We have fallen short of God's righteous standard,[24] are alienated from him[25] and deserve his just condemnation.[26] Moreover, we ourselves are incapable of putting right this situation which we have brought about by our sin.

The Bible goes on to show that what we cannot do for ourselves God has done for us in Christ. He stepped in to remove the barrier caused by our sin and to restore us to fellowship with God.[27] Christ, by dying and rising on our behalf, has cleansed us from the guilt of sin. The Bible then goes further, showing us that salvation has positive as well as negative aspects, for we are not only saved *from* sin, but saved *for* life. So Christians are described as those who have been 'born again'[28] and who have already laid hold of eternal life.[29] Moreover, the Holy Spirit now at work in Christians is transforming them into the kind of people that God has always intended them to be.[30]

In contrast, the Divine Light Mission has nothing to say about sin and its consequences and cure. It cannot provide the power to live the kind of life that God requires. Instead of the assurance of eternal life in Christ, received as God's gift through faith, it offers only an emotional and intellect-denying experience with a discredited Guru and an event-

---

[23] Genesis 1:26; *etc*.   [24] Romans 3:23.   [25] Ephesians 2:1ff.
[26] Romans 6:23.   [27] Ephesians 2:4ff.   [28] John 3:1ff.
[29] John 5:24, *etc*.   [30] Galatians 5:22ff.

ual escape from rebirth by absorption into Cosmic Energy.

Scripture
The Divine Light Mission believes that 'all scriptures glorify the divine Knowledge' and its members are happy to give equal validity to the sacred writings of Christians, Hindus, Muslims, Sikhs, Taoists and Buddhists. Mission members maintain that what all religions have been seeking after and what all their devotees have written about in their scriptures, has now found a contemporary fulfilment in Guru Maharaj Ji. This is another clear point of departure between Christians and the Divine Light Mission. Christians believe uncompromisingly that God's full and final revelation of himself has been given to the world in Christ, the incarnate Word, and that this revelation is contained in the Bible, the written Word. This is the significance of passages such as Hebrews 1 to which we have referred already.

It follows, therefore, that Christians believe that the Bible contains everything necessary for salvation, and that for them the teaching of the Bible must always be the yardstick against which all religious claims have to be tested. True religion is biblical religion. It follows that although Christians may sometimes read the sacred writings of other religions with interest, they will not expect to find in them anything which they do not already possess fully in Christ. For Christians, the Bible must always be the authoritative guide in matters of faith and practice. This scriptural yardstick is particularly important when any religious sect claims, as the Divine Light Mission is claiming, to give a direct experience of God.

The Guru
The most important area of conflict between the views of the Divine Light Mission and the Christian Faith, however, concern the person of Guru Maharaj Ji. As we have seen, the Guru's devotees believe that he is to people today what Jesus Christ was to people living two thousand years ago. Whereas Jesus was *their* Saviour, Lord and Master, Guru Maharaj Ji is *our* Saviour, Lord and Master. Just as Jesus

was *their* incarnation of the divine, so the Guru is *our* incarnation of the divine. The early Christians opened their hearts to Jesus. Today's people must open their hearts to Guru Maharaj Ji. In other words, in the Divine Light Mission's system of belief, the young Guru has taken the place that Jesus Christ occupies in mainstream Christianity.

At this point there can be no room for any kind of compromise. We cannot serve Christ and the Guru. If we believe that Jesus is the Son of God sent by his Father to be the Saviour of the world, we shall not want any alternative saviour. If we are ready to confess 'Jesus Christ is Lord',[31] we shall be profoundly disturbed by anyone asking us to say that Guru Maharaj Ji is Lord.

The idea that the Guru is to people today what Jesus was to people of his day, is in direct conflict with the teaching of the New Testament, where we are told that God's progressive revelation of himself down through the ages has reached its culmination in the Person of Jesus Christ. So we read in Hebrews 1:1, for example,

> When in former times God spoke to our forefathers, he spoke in fragmentary and varied fashion through the prophets. But in this the final age he has spoken to us in the Son . . . who is the effulgence of God's splendour and the stamp of God's very being.

Therefore, if we take the New Testament seriously, the claims about Guru Maharaj Ji are not only unscriptural, but blasphemous.

Summary of main differences

Divine Light Mission	*Christianity*

God

| Impersonal. 'Cosmic Energy'. 'Universal Mind'. | There is one God, yet within the unity of the |

---

[31] Philippians 2:11.

Godhead there are three divine Persons, Father, Son and Holy Spirit.

The Saviour

As the twentieth-century incarnation (avatar) of God, Guru Maharaj Ji is fulfilling the same role for people today that Jesus fulfilled 2,000 years ago. Guru Maharaj Ji has replaced Jesus as the contemporary saviour.

Jesus was and is the only Saviour for all mankind. 'There is no salvation in anyone else at all, for there is no other name under heaven granted to men, by which we may receive salvation' (Acts 4:12).

Salvation

Salvation means release from the endless cycle of birth, death and rebirth, and absorption into Ultimate Reality. This is achieved by means of the direct 'knowledge' or experience of God given through Guru Maharaj Ji.

Salvation means not only deliverance from the guilt, power and consequences of sin but also new birth into a fullness of life which God gives through Christ.

Authority

Guru Maharaj Ji speaks for God. All the scriptures of the world's religions may be used to 'glorify the Divine Knowledge', but they are also subordinate to the Guru and are not used in any sense to test the validity of his claims.

God's full and final revelation of himself has been given to the world in Jesus Christ, the incarnate Word, and is contained in the Bible, God's written Word. The Bible speaks with the authority of God, therefore, and is the yardstick by which to measure all claims to religious truth.

91

6 Transcendental Meditation

According to its leader, the Maharishi Mahesh Yogi,

> Transcendental meditation is a natural technique which allows the conscious mind to experience increasingly more subtle states of thought until the source of thought, the unlimited reservoir of energy and creative intelligence, is reached. This simple practice expands the capacity of the conscious mind and a man is able to use his full potential in all fields of thought and action.[1]

Other exponents of the art of what they call 'tranquility without pills' have defined Transcendental Meditation more briefly as 'a mental process that prepares an individual for activity as well as relieving accumulated stress and providing a period of deep rest'.[2] Meanwhile, the movement's posters proclaim that 'Transcendental Meditation is a natural spontaneous technique which allows each individual to expand his conscious mind and improve all aspects of life'.

In line with some public pronouncements by its guru, the TM movement claims that it is not religious, has no theological presuppositions, makes no ethical demands and requires none of its members to change his life-style. It is merely a technique, practised at least two thousand years before Christ, which many ancient teachers have handed

[1] Cited by Jhan Robbins and David Fisher in *Tranquility Without Pills* (Souvenir Press, 1973), p. 20.   [2] *Ibid.*, p. 170.

down, which Jesus himself used, and which has as its goal making people happy.

Despite such frequent disclaimers, it will be argued in this chapter that TM is a modern religious movement. It will be pointed out that, given its present impetus by an Indian guru in the bhakti tradition of Hinduism, it operates within a Hindu philosophical framework, uses Hindu mantras, and addresses itself to Hindu deities. That is why, in October 1977, a New Jersey law court ruled that TM could no longer be taught in the state's schools, for of course United States law forbids the teaching of religion in its schools. Similarly, that is why TM appears as a chapter in this book about modern religious alternatives to orthodox Christianity.

The guru of Transcendental Meditation

If one accepts the Maharishi's claim that he is simply handing on to the world what has been widely practised for about four hundred years, it is incorrect to call him the founder of TM. Nevertheless, none can doubt that because of his activities as TM's chief propagator and guru in the last twenty years, the Maharishi Mahesh Yogi has become almost a household name, especially in America where he now claims a very substantial following. Only five feet tall, with a long scraggy white beard, piercing eyes, and usually dressed in a white silk dhoti, he has proved the most unlikely of the successful religious leaders of modern times.

Born in 1918 as the third of four children of a forest ranger, he was called Mahesh Prasad Varma, before his spiritual enlightenment led him to change his name to the Maharishi Mahesh Yogi. Translated roughly, his new name means 'Great Sage of the family of Mahesh who practises yoga'. After graduating in physics from Allahabad University in 1942, the Maharishi worked for five years in a factory, during which time he taught himself Sanskrit. Then at the end of the Second World War he withdrew into the seclusion of the Himalayan foothills to meditate for the next thirteen years. His mentor was a Hindu swami named Brahmananda Saraswati, who is now known within the

TM movement as Guru Dev, 'divine teacher', and who is addressed alongside Hindu deities in TM initiation ceremonies.

In 1959 the Maharishi emerged with what we now know as Transcendental Meditation, a technique which he believed would revolutionize the world and put an end to warfare. Finding little response to his teaching in his native India, where gurus have never been in short supply, he announced a nine-year plan for spreading his teaching throughout the world. Believing that the West would quickly respond to his teaching and encourage the growth of his new movement, he then moved to London, where he founded the International Meditation Society.

The Maharishi laboured for about eight years without achieving any appreciable success. Then in 1967 came a remarkable breakthrough. He met George Harrison, one of the Beatles, who had been studying Indian music. Harrison was so impressed by this vegetarian celibate with his captivating smile and message of peace and tranquillity that he persuaded the rest of his group that the Maharishi had what they were all looking for. The four of them went to Wales with the guru, where he introduced them to his ideas and taught them to meditate. For a short time they remained enthusiastic disciples, claiming that in him they had found the answer to their needs and had begun to live. Other show-business personalities, including the Rolling Stones, and many other people, were suitably impressed. Hundreds began practising meditation the Maharishi way, paying him a week's salary for his instruction in the art.

For a time it seemed as if the Maharishi had achieved lasting fame. Through the publicity received through his association with the Beatles he had acquired world-wide popularity and a steady income. 'Half the world seemed to feel that this Eastern guru could whip up instant happiness as easily as a morning cup of instant coffee.'[3]

The claims the Maharishi made for his technique were not modest ones. By following his natural, simple and non-

[3] William J. Petersen, *Those Curious New Cults*, p. 188.

religious method of meditation, he maintained, the lives of individuals would be perfectly fulfilled and lasting peace would be spread throughout the world. Indeed, if one-tenth of the world's population could be persuaded to practise TM, meditating regularly twice a day, war would not be known on earth for centuries to come. He explained the reason for such optimism. It was inner tension in the lives of individuals which led to conflict, so if the tension went, war would disappear with it. Similarly, tension led to all kinds of sickness, so if people faithfully applied his techniques the world's hospitals would be emptied.

Then TM suffered a severe setback, for the Beatles, who had been instrumental in bringing the Maharishi to the notice of millions, decided that they had made a mistake and that his message and techniques were not the answer to their needs. Others who had jumped on to the band-wagon soon found their excuses to get off, and, following a disastrous American tour, the Maharishi became disillusioned with the fickleness of western society. He returned to India, admitting, 'I know that I have failed. My mission is over', vowing never to return to the West.

Nevertheless, back in India he began to develop his organization in a business-like way. It became such a financial success that the authorities began to take an interest, so in 1970 the Maharishi moved his headquarters to Italy, and then to Spain.

His work, which has seen a remarkable revival over the last few years, is now conducted according to another World Plan. He aims to set up many teacher-training centres (destined eventually to become TM universities) in order to bring to everyone everywhere the means of realizing individual potential. TM now seems to be a prosperous movement and in 1978 was able to acquire, as its main British centre, Mentmore Towers in Buckinghamshire, for some £250,000. There are said to be a million Transcendental Meditationists in the USA, with another 300,000 initiates joining each month, whilst in Britain the monthly recruitment figure is about 900. No figures are known for the drop-out rate, though some opponents say it is high. TM operates also under the names of other organizations, such as the Spiritual Regeneration Movement and the Students International Meditation Society.

The techniques of Transcendental Meditation

We have seen that TM claims to be simply a technique, not a system of belief.

> Leaders of the TM movement are quick to point out that their technique is not in any way similar to a religion. Nor is it intended to replace any religious beliefs. If anything, it acts to strengthen an individual's belief.[4]

Transcendental Meditationists are, they say, simply passing on a well-tried method of meditation, which has been handed down through many centuries and which, in our day, finds its chief expression and best exponent in the Maharishi Mahesh Yogi, who himself learnt it from Guru Dev.

Against that claim, this chapter has maintained that the techniques of TM operate within a Hindu framework, and against a Hindu philosophical background, involve the constant use of Hindu mantras, and include attitudes of reverence towards Hindu deities. TM is, therefore, a religious movement. In weighing this argument it is necessary to look in some detail at what is involved in the practice of TM. It will then be possible to consider the philosophical presuppositions that lie behind it.

The Maharishi's disciples claim that their movement's remarkable growth stems from the word-of-mouth testimony of satisfied customers. They say that the lives of those practising TM are so obviously improved that their relatives, friends and neighbours are suitably impressed and that this then makes it easier to persuade other people also to give TM a fair trial. Interested contacts are then invited to attend public lectures to learn what is being offered through TM and what they have to do to obtain it. This

---

[4] Robbins and Fisher, *op. cit.*, p. 22.

is the chief method of bringing people into the movement, though newspaper advertising encourages others to attend the lectures.

Before proceeding to initiation into Transcendental Meditation, people are required to attend these public lectures, which are given by Maharishi-trained teachers. Usually there are two such introductory lectures, which aim to outline the possibilities open to all who practise TM and begin to explain in an elementary way the mechanics involved in the technique itself. It is claimed that the majority of those who pass the first hurdle, and actually attend public lectures, go on to accept the lecturers' invitation to make appointments for initiation – the puja ceremony.

The person wishing to be initiated is given a date and time when he is to return for this ceremony. He is told to bring with him three pieces of fruit, six fresh flowers, a clean white handkerchief and his fee. Members say that these objects have no practical use in themselves. They are merely part of a traditional ceremony and are to TM what wigs are to English barristers.[5] Practical or not, the offerings are highly symbolic, the flowers representing life, the fruit the seed of life, and the handkerchief the cleansing of the spirit. When the candidate arrives, duly bearing these objects, he takes off his shoes and enters a simple room. There he finds a table bearing a picture of Guru Dev (the Maharishi's teacher). Incense is burning and the room is lit by candles.

The twofold purpose of the puja ceremony of initiation has been set out clearly by two authors who are themselves active members of the TM movement.[6] The first object is to impress upon the initiate the fact that he is following in a great and ancient tradition. So there is an invocation in Sanskrit, referring to great teachers of the past; and the whole ceremony takes place in a solemn atmosphere. The second object is to remind the teacher performing the initiation that he is only handing down a tradition which he himself has been taught. Because of the use of Sanskrit, however, it is unlikely that the initiate will have any clear

[5] *Ibid.*, p. 55.   [6] *Ibid.*, p. 59.

knowledge of what is being said on this occasion.

The ceremony begins with the teacher who sings a Sanskrit ritual. Having been told that TM is not a religion, it sometimes surprises initiates when they discover that this ritual has been addressed to several traditional Hindu deities, such as Brahma, Vishnu and Krishna; and that included among this distinguished company is Guru Dev, who has presumably been deified because of all that he was able to do for the Maharishi. It is in this context that the initiate then receives his mantra and is instructed in the art of TM.

The mantra, a Sanskrit word, is given to the initiate secretly and he is told not to share it with anyone else. It is claimed within the movement that every new member is given a mantra that is especially suitable for him. In practice, the number of such mantras is limited, there being about sixteen of them. They seem to be allocated to new members simply on the basis of their age when joining. Thus someone between 16 and 17 would be given the mantra 'Ema', another between 22 and 23 would receive 'Ienga', and a 35 to 39 year old would be allocated 'Kirim'. Though said to be meaningless sounds, used merely as part of the TM technique, mantras are in fact related to specific Hindu deities. When he meditates using the mantra, therefore, the newly initiated member is in reality (though usually in ignorance) addressing a Hindu deity.

After his initiation, when he will have practised meditation under his teacher's supervision, the new member of the movement will have several more meetings with his teacher. Together with other initiates, he will receive further instruction and be encouraged to share his first experiences of TM. As with the other sects examined in this book, the importance of the group cannot be over-emphasized. Although meditation is essentially an individual exercise, the support the new meditator receives from other meditators is often crucial, particularly in the early stages when there are problems to be ironed out and doubts to be removed.

But what happens in meditation the TM way? Meditators are told that they are to allow their minds to go into neutral and let themselves be brought into tune with the universe. 'The thing about meditation', two members of the TM movement explain, 'is not to concentrate, but to take the reins off your mind and let it run anywhere it wants.'[7] Meditators must 'avoid concentrating on anything in particular. Concentration holds the mind at one level and will not allow it to submerge into a deeper level of consciousness'.[8] Readers knowing their own minds may raise their eyebrows at such advice, but there is no doubt about what is intended.

> Inevitably, according to the Maharishi, when you let your mind wander freely it will drift in the direction of things that please you greatly. If eating a rare filet mignon is what makes you happiest, a picture of a juicy steak may pop into your head. Or you may find yourself thinking about the last time you made love. Or you may remember a long-forgotten snowball fight. The important thing is not to direct your mind in any specific direction.[9]

The purpose of such undirected meditation is explained. It is to make the meditator's life more fulfilling, to give him deep rest, and then to make him more energetically active. So the goal is a fuller life. It is explained that normally we live on three levels of consciousness, namely waking, sleeping and dreaming. There are, however, other important levels of consciousness which we can achieve only through TM. These are transcendental consciousness, cosmic consciousness, God consciousness, unity consciousness and brahman consciousness, though most TM members concern themselves only with the first two and perhaps do not even know about the last three. These latter phases are for the 'high fliers', those with years of TM experience behind them.

Transcendental consciousness has been defined as 'a fourth state of consciousness, which is differentiated by the body being in a state of physical rest but the mind being

[7] *Ibid.*, p. 62.   [8] *Ibid.*, p. 37.   [9] *Ibid.*

awake. Also known as "restful alertness". Differs substantially from the common states of consciousness in many physical ways.'[10] 'Physically, I felt a wave of relaxation surging through my body', one meditator explains.[11] It is also called the transcendental state of being.

Cosmic consciousness is the next stage. It means being able to remain at the 'state of being' on a conscious level and on a permanent basis. According to the Maharishi, the meditator is then beyond all seeing, hearing, touching, smelling and tasting – beyond all thinking and beyond all feeling. 'This state of the unmanifested, absolute, pure consciousness of Being is the ultimate state of life.'[12] When he has achieved cosmic consciousness, a person is truly happy, it is explained, for all stress has disappeared.[13] In the Maharishi's thought, then, it seems that almost imperceptibly cosmic consciousness gradually moves into, or merges with, the other three higher states of being until, as in classical Hindu thought, the individual loses himself in ultimate reality.

For the average member, however, the theory is unknown territory. He is instructed to practise TM, not to think about it. And for those who do practise it, TM makes some impressive claims. Twice-a-day meditation the TM way is said to provide more deep rest than an entire night's sleep. It claims to provide cures for psychological disorders, drug addiction and alcoholism. It can help a person to overcome the smoking habit, aid him in his efforts to lose weight, improve his sex life, increase his energy and efficiency, lower his blood pressure, give him better all-round health and stability, and so make him a happy and fulfilled person.

Apart from such benefits accruing to the individual, TM also claims remarkable results for the world at large if its message is applied. As we noted earlier, the Maharishi actually maintained that if a tenth of the world's population adopted TM there would be no wars, for the tensions causing conflict would have been removed.

Others tell a different story. In an article in the *Guardian* on 15 August 1979, Stephen Cook referred to a number of

---

[10] *Ibid.*, pp. 170f.   [11] *Ibid.*, p. 160.   [12] *Ibid.*, p. 40.   [13] *Ibid.*, p. 47.

disillusioned former disciples who no longer supported the Maharishi. They listed a number of complaints. Some said that despite years of meditation they had never succeeded in achieving the promised levitation. Moreover, far from solving all their problems. TM had led some of them to 'intensive depression, suicidal feelings, inability to work, and back, digestive or gynaecological ailments'. Others had become alarmed at the effects of TM on their friends. 'There were all the signs of classical spirit possession', claimed London barrister, Hester Fishberg, who had herself been in the movement for five years and had become one of its official teachers.

Opinions are, therefore, divided about the alleged beneficial effects of TM; and even among those who have tasted and at first enjoyed what the Maharishi has to offer, a significant number have afterwards left the movement unsatisfied. Maybe the secret of whatever success there has been for TM techniques could have been achieved equally well by any method requiring participants to stop rushing around and to be quiet and still for short periods every morning and evening. Such an assessment is supported by the more recent researches of Dr H. Benson, associate professor at Harvard Medical School. Some years ago he supported the claims of TM and the results of his research then published are still used to bolster the movement's claims. Today, however, he believes that other forms of meditation work equally well.[14]

Transcendental Meditation and Christianity

There are a number of very important questions to ask regarding the nature of TM and about its relationship with Christianity. As we have seen, TM specifically denies that it is a religion or that it has much in common with any religion. As a technique helping individuals towards fulfilment, it claims to encourage its members to be better followers of whatever religion they profess. All the evidence, however, points in a different direction, as we shall see as

[14] *The Relaxation Response.*

101

we look more carefully at the TM initiation ceremony and at the states of consciousness said to be achieved through the practice of TM as well as the philosophical presuppositions forming the framework in which TM operates.

The initiation ceremony is said to be a simple recognition of the debt that present-day meditators owe to the great teachers of the technique who existed in past ages and who handed it on to this generation. But this claim just does not stand up to close examination. The ceremony is a puja, conducted in reverence and in Sanskrit, one of the sacred languages of Hinduism. As the initiate enters barefoot, his attention is drawn towards a table on which has been placed a picture of Guru Dev, now believed to be divine. Incense and candles are burning. It is hard to believe that any objective outsider would regard all this as anything other than a religious atmosphere.

What can only be described as an act of adoration then takes place. It is directed towards various Hindu deities and after the recital of each of their names the teacher says, 'I bow down.' There is a specific reference to 'the whole galaxy of the gods'. Many of the invocations of this prayer are addressed to Guru Dev. One reads,

White as camphor, kindness incarnate, the essence of creation garlanded with Brahman, ever dwelling in the lotus of my heart, the creative impulse of cosmic life, to That, in the form of *Guru Dev*, I bow down.

Later the prayer continues,

Guru in the glory of *Brahma*, *Guru* in the glory of *Vishnu*, *Guru* in the glory of the great *Lord Shiva*, *Guru* in the glory of the personified transcendental fulness of *Brahman*, to Him, to *Shri Guru Dev* adorned with glory, I bow down.[15]

There is more in similar vein, Guru Dev being described

---

[15] Cited by Pat Means in *The Mystical Maze* (Campus Crusade for Christ, 1976), p. 245.

as the 'Self-Sufficient', 'the embodiment of pure knowledge which is beyond and above the universe like the sky', 'the One, the Eternal, the Pure, the Immovable ... whose status transcends thought'.[16] According to Pat Means, 'This translation is from a secret uncopyrighted TM handbook called *The Holy Tradition*, p. 5. It is given only to those who qualify to teach and to be initiators for TM training'.[17]

Now whatever else may be said about the initiation invocation, and Christians will obviously wish to say something, it is patently obvious that here we are dealing with religion. Not only does the teacher address Hindu deities, acknowledging the need to offer them his devotion, but he also addresses Guru Dev in such a way as to make it clear that, in line with Hindu thought, he believes that in some real sense this former teacher of the Maharishi is now an embodiment of the divine, an avatar, an incarnation.

During his initiatory puja, the initiate brings his offerings of fruit, flowers and a white handkerchief, as well as his fee for initiation which may be the equivalent of a week's income. We need not concern ourselves overmuch with the financial transaction. In an age when people are expected to pay a fairly substantial price to watch football, to have a hair-do, or to go out for a modest meal, we should not be surprised at the willingness of some to pay a week's salary for initiation into a technique which promises to give them complete self-fulfilment. If such a state can be achieved with money it is cheap at the price. What ought to concern us more is to whom the fruit, flowers and white handkerchief are being offered, and what is the purpose. It has been pointed out that those belonging to the TM movement explain that the flowers represent life, the fruit the seed of the life, and the handkerchief the cleansing of the spirit. Again, it is hard to escape the conclusion that here we are dealing with religion, and not merely a traditional secular ceremony in honour of past benefactors – especially when we view these offerings in the context of the invocatory prayer referred to previously.

The use of the mantras points us in the same direction.

[16] *Ibid.*   [17] *Ibid.*, p. 246.

Although the movement claims that they are meaningless words, nothing more than sounds to aid people in meditation, and although there is some evidence from other forms of meditation of the use of similar techniques, the New Jersey court case referred to earlier produced evidence from a former TM teacher showing that the mantras used in TM have traditionally been used to symbolize specific Hindu deities.[18] Whether he believes it or not, therefore, the person using a mantra for the purpose of meditation is engaging in a religious act, for the focus of his meditation is a Hindu god.

Moving on to the various states of consciousness into which TM is said to take its users, it would seem almost impossible for anyone (except those who have accepted the TM propaganda that the movement is non-religious) to view cosmic consciousness and the subsequent states of God consciousness, unity consciousness and brahman consciousness in anything but religious terms. The Maharishi, true to his Hindu upbringing, sees salvation in terms of complete absorption in the divine. Indeed, in this respect (as in others) his views are similar to those of another Indian guru whose views are considered elsewhere in this book, Guru Maharaj Ji, who believes that man achieves his bliss, mokshya, liberation, nirvana, salvation, or samadhi (call it what you will), when his mind is in exact accord with the Universal Mind.

Now the Maharishi must know, as must any of his followers who have the slightest acquaintance with Hinduism, that such teaching stems from the rather sophisticated type of Hinduism found in the *Upanishads*, where doctrine revolves around the two key words, brahman and atman. Brahman stands for ultimate reality, atman for the individual self or soul. According to these sacred writings of Hinduism, the ideal is that the individual self (atman) should be at one with ultimate reality (brahman). This unity, however, is not seen in terms of a personal relationship, but rather as the absorption of the individual in 'God'. He is then like a drop of water lost in a bucketful. He no longer

[18] *Ibid.*, pp. 247ff.

exists as an individual in his own right. It is not difficult to see the close relationship between those ideas and the Maharishi's teaching about the higher levels of consciousness which culminate in brahman consciousness.

Whether or not the Maharishi wishes to identify his views so closely as I have done with the religion of the *Upanishads*, it seems to me beyond dispute that TM uses religious language, involves its members (with or without their knowledge) in religious worship, and directs those who use its techniques towards the goal of Indian religion. No matter how often the Maharishi says TM is not a religion, therefore, it is as religious as any of the other sects considered in this book.

That being the case, one may wish to ask why the Maharishi is so determined to hide the fact. One can only assume that it is because he believes it will get a more favourable reception from western society (where at present he appears to be concentrating his efforts) if it dresses itself in the garb of a non-religious, quasi-scientific and psychological technology. If this is the case, one can only hope that the increased publicity TM is now receiving from both supporters and opponents will encourage the Maharishi to come clean and admit that his movement is a sect of Hinduism in the bhakti tradition. Then at least people will know what it is they are either accepting or rejecting, and surely that cannot but be good for all concerned, whatever their final decision about the movement.

From a Christian point of view, something more needs to be said. It most urgently needs to be said to those professing Christians who have taken up the practice of TM, believing it to be wholly compatible with their Christian faith. After looking closely at what is involved in TM initiation and what is the final goal of TM, it is clear that TM and the Christian faith are poles apart and that no-one can honestly embrace the one without being disloyal to the other.

Because the initiation puja involves the worship of Hindu deities, and because the use of the mantras implies approach to such deities for help, Christians have no choice but to regard TM as idolatrous.

Because embracing the movement involves recognizing Guru Dev as a divine incarnation, Christians have no choice but to regard TM as blasphemous.

And because following the TM way of salvation requires no acknowledgement of sin, no offering of repentance, no reception of grace, no Christ, no cross, no resurrection and no regeneration, Christians have no choice but to regard TM as erroneous.

That is not to say, of course, that everyone involved in TM lacks sincerity, or that the movement has not much to say to a western society so intent on chasing material prosperity that it has forgotten the injunction, 'Be still and know that I am God.' When all this has readily been admitted, however, it still needs to be said loudly and clearly that TM is a sect of the Hindu religion and that, as such, there is much in it which is incompatible with Christianity.[19]

Summary of main differences

Transcendental Meditation	*Christianity*
Religion	
TM claims not to be a religion, but all its philosophical pre-suppositions are Hinduistic in origin.	Claims to be a religion based on God's revelation of himself in Jesus Christ as recorded in the Bible.
God	
Despite the disclaimer about religion, its initiation ceremony and its use of mantras in meditation techniques are all directed towards Hindu deities such as Brahma, Vishnu and Shiva.	Believes in God revealed in the Bible as Father, Son and Holy Spirit, three Persons within the unity of the Godhead.

[19] For further reading see John Allan, *TM: A Cosmic Confidence Trick* (IVP, 1980).

This is seen in terms of freedom from inner tensions through the techniques of meditation. The successive goals are transcendental consciousness, cosmic consciousness, God consciousness, unity consciousness and brahman consciousness. The ultimate aim is absorption into the divine.

Christianity sees man's basic problem to be alienation from God through sin. Salvation, achieved for all by Christ but appropriated individually by faith, not only frees from the guilt, power and consequence of sin, but also introduces the believer to a new life in Christ.

7. The Hare Krishna movement

More correctly described as the International Society for Krishna Consciousness (ISKCON for short), the Hare Krishna movement is one of the most colourful of the sects examined in this book. Unashamedly Hindu in its allegiance, though working mainly in the western world, it requires its devotees to wear distinctive dress, its men to shave their heads, and all who embrace its teaching to adopt an ascetic life-style. Though coming from the same religious background as Transcendental Meditation and the Divine Light Mission, therefore, and like both of them owing its current impetus to an Indian guru, it is more demanding than either.

It claims a modest membership of some 10,000 devotees in the USA and a few more thousands in other parts of the world. Members are often active in large cities such as New York, London, Rome, Paris, Amsterdam and Ottawa. They are aggressively evangelistic in their service of the Hindu god Krishna and are expected to devote the whole of their lives to the spread of Krishna consciousness throughout the world.

The founder of the Hare Krishna Movement

This Hindu sect owes its existence to a man now known to his followers as His Divine Grace A. C. Bhaktivedanta Swami Prabhupada, who died recently in his eighties, and who founded the International Society for Krishna Consciousness in New York in 1965. He was born in Calcutta in 1896 and studied Philosophy, English and Economics at the university of that city. In 1922 he met a Hindu guru, Siddartha Goswami, who taught him about Krishna consciousness. Eleven years later Prabhupada was formally initiated as Goswami's disciple, and, encouraged by his master, began writing a commentary on the Indian spiritual classic, the *Bhagavad-Gita*. He remained in his home town until 1950, studying, writing, and for a time working in the pharmaceutical industry. Then he decided to drop out of society to pursue his religious aims, forsaking not only his work but also his wife and five children. His followers say he 'retired from family life'.

Prabhupada's spiritual master, Goswami, had himself abandoned a university professorship for the same purpose. Goswami had based his ideas on the teaching of the fifteenth-century Indian sage, Chaitanya, who had popularized the idea that Krishna was supreme among the Hindu gods and ought therefore to be given man's complete devotion. It was Goswami, so Prabhupada says, who commissioned him with the task of spreading knowledge of Krishna to the western world. Obedient to the guru, in 1965 Prabhupada left India for the United States where, practically penniless, he began his missionary work in and around New York.

Wearing a saffron robe in the style of the Indian holy man, Prabhupada began preaching his message of Krishna. He directed his work mainly towards young people, challenging them to drop out of the rat race of modern society, to turn their backs on the illusions of materialism, and to devote themselves to the love and lifelong service of Krishna. Some accepted the challenge, particularly a number who had been on drugs, and joined him to form a cult of Krishna worship in a disused New York store. As was the case with Transcendental Meditation, the movement was given some impetus by the temporary support of George Harrison, one of the Beatles. Following that example, many others quickly 'flocked to the grandfather figure in the saffron robes'.[1]

[1] Pat Means, *The Mystical Maze*, p. 148.

After the founding of the International Society for Krishna Consciousness in July 1966, the movement spread to San Francisco and then to many other cities in the USA and Europe. Encouraged by the response, in 1968 Prabhupada started an experimental farming community in the hills of West Virginia, this being the first of such communities in the USA and farther afield. Then in 1972 he turned his attention to education, founding the Gurukula School in Texas. The following years saw the founding of international centres in India, where devotees from the West could stay to gain first-hand experience of Indian culture. Prabhupada's writings are published by his own Bhaktivedanta Book Trust, which was founded in 1972. His followers say that their leader 'circled the globe twelve times on lecture tours that have taken him to six continents'.[2] His movement now operates in about seventy centres through the world, and is particularly active in urban areas.

'His Divine Grace' was regarded by his followers, not only as 'the world's most distinguished scholar and teacher of Vedic religion and philosophy', but also as 'the latest representative in a line of succession, originating with Lord Krishna, through which Vedic knowledge is transmitted'.[3] They treated him with great reverence and some of them appeared to believe that he was divine.

The beliefs of the Hare Krishna movement

The beliefs of the Hare Krishna movement have to be seen against the background of the Hindu religion from which the movement originates. In particular, they need to be seen in the light of Hindu beliefs about ultimate reality, the physical world, karma and reincarnation, and salvation.

Although acknowledging a whole galaxy of deities, popular Hinduism has settled for a 'trinity' of Brahman the Creator, Vishnu the Preserver and Shiva the Destroyer. Vishnu, so it is believed, has manifested himself in a num-

---

[2] *Bhagavad-Gita As It Is* (The Bhaktivedanta Book Trust, New York, 1972), p. 276. [3] *Ibid.*, cover.

110

ber of forms, sometimes as animals and sometimes in human form. The animal avatars have included a fish, a bear, a turtle and a lion, whilst the human manifestations have been as Rama, Buddha and Krishna. A more sophisticated tradition within Hinduism, on the other hand, thought of Ultimate Reality, Brahman, in impersonal terms, and thought that man's highest ambition was to lose his individuality (atman) in the impersonality of the deity.

As noted earlier, the beliefs of the Hare Krishna movement have been derived indirectly from the teaching of the Indian sage Chaitanya, who not only rejected the idea of God's impersonality but went further than many of his contemporaries in teaching that Krishna was not only one of the incarnations of Vishnu but was, in fact, supreme among all the gods. Following Chaitanya, there has been a steady tradition within Hinduism of devotion to Krishna. The Hare Krishna movement is a modern example of that view.

The most important doctrine of the Hare Krishna movement is, therefore, belief in the supremacy of Krishna over all other gods within the Hindu galaxy. Commenting on a passage in the *Bhagavad-Gita*, Prabhupada writes,

> He is the Supreme Personality of Godhead. No living entity, including Brahma, Lord Shiva, or even Narayana, can possess opulence as fully as Krishna . . . No one is equal to or above Him. He is the primeval Lord . . . And He is the supreme cause of all causes . . . the Absolute Truth.[4]

He adds that Krishna is 'alive in the heart of every living entity'.[5]

Unlike the school of thought which views God as impersonal and sees the individual's ultimate destiny as to be lost in Ultimate Reality, Prabhupada and his disciples believe that the individual soul is also eternal.[6] The founder of the Hare Krishna movement asserts that the *Bhagavad-Gita*, which he regards as authoritative scripture, does not support the impersonal theory that after liberation the in-

[4] *Ibid.*, pp. 17f.   [5] *Ibid.*, p. 22.   [6] *Ibid.*, p. 23.

dividual soul will merge with the impersonal brahman and no longer continue its individual existence.[7] So, following the lead of this epic poem (which one writer has described as perhaps the greatest religious document of Hinduism), the Hare Krishna movement stresses the importance of a personal relationship with Krishna based on love.

Another strong Hindu tradition finding modern support in the Hare Krishna movement is that of maya, the view that apart from ultimate spiritual reality all else is illusion, the fruit of ignorance. 'It is like the desert mirage, appearance and not reality, which vanishes with a nearer approach.'[8] This applies in particular to the physical world that surrounds the individual and provides his illusory environment. What the enlightened person does, therefore, is to recognize this unreality for what it is. Only then will he find his true self.

Statements by Prabhupada need to be understood in the light of such teaching.

> Persons who are led by the material conception of life do not know that the aim of life is realization of the Absolute Truth . . . Such persons are captivated by the external features of the material world, and therefore they do not know what liberation is.[9]

Because of this view, he is able to go on to describe attachment to family life, wife and children as 'skin disease'.[10] One must assume, also, that this was how he justified his action in forsaking his own wife and children and how the movement now justifies its own encouragement of devotees to forsake home, family and job in the search for Krishna consciousness. As Prabhupada explains,

> A sincere devotee of the Lord learns to hate all material sense enjoyment due to his higher taste for spiritual enjoyment in the association of the Lord.[11]

[7] *Ibid.*
[8] Ninian Smart, *The Religious Experience of Mankind* (Collins Fontana Library, 1971), p. 22.
[9] *Bhagavad-Gita As It Is*, p. 18.   [10] *Ibid.*, p. 21.   [11] *Ibid.*, p. 39.

Also within Hinduism there is a strong belief in reincarnation or, more correctly, the transmigration of souls, and linked with this is the doctrine of karma. In brief, the idea is that every activity of thought or conduct, good or bad, sets in motion a series of consequences, a chain reaction, just as a stone thrown in a pond results in an ever-expanding circle of ripples. This is the law of karma. Depending upon the kind of karma a person has built up in his present life, he will be reborn to either a higher or a lower level of existence. In other words, the eternal soul will pursue this restless kind of existence after existence until, perhaps, in time, he will achieve liberation – that is, freedom from such existence for ever.[12]

The view of Prabhupada and his followers are strictly in line with such teaching. After referring to the verse in the *Bhagavad-Gita* which says of the eternal soul, 'He takes one kind of body and again quits it to take another', the leader of the Hare Krishna movement comments as follows: 'If he likes, he can change his body to a higher grade, and if he likes, he can move to a lower class.'[13] In case people misunderstand the phrase 'If he likes', however, he explains:

At the time of death, the consciousness he has created will carry him on to the next type of body. If he has made his consciousness like that of a cat or dog, he is sure to change from his human body to a cat's or a dog's body. If he has fixed his consciousness on godly qualities he will change into the form of a demigod. And if he changes his consciousness into Krishna consciousness, he will be transferred to Krishnaloka in the spiritual world and will be with Krishna.[14]

Elsewhere Krishnaloka is defined as 'Krishna's eternal abode',[15] and as a 'supreme planet in the spiritual sky'.[16]

This brings us to the Hindu views of salvation. As seen earlier, there are two main views, depending upon whether

[12] Sir Norman Anderson, *The World's Religions* (IVP, ⁴1975), pp. 142ff.
[13] *Bhagavad-Gita As It Is*, pp. 230f.
[14] *Ibid.*, p. 313.   [15] *Ibid.*, p. 281.   [16] *Ibid.*, p. 313.

their advocates believe in a personal or impersonal deity. For the impersonalists, salvation is seen as release from the illusion of the physical world and union with Ultimate Reality. Then, like a drop of water in a bucketful, the individual is lost in the Absolute and ceases to exist as an individual in his own right. For the personalists, salvation is still seen as release from the physical world, that is from the endless chain of life, death, rebirth, but the destiny of the soul is to be in union with a god who is seen in personal terms.

The Hare Krishna movement stands quite clearly in this second tradition. For the eternal soul who achieves his liberation by means of Krishna consciousness, there awaits the eternal bliss of being at one with (though still in a sense distinct from) Krishna, the Supreme Personality, the Lord whom he has loved and served before deliverance was achieved.

We must now look carefully at the way the movement believes that such eternal bliss is to be achieved. As we shall see, it is essentially a 'do-it-yourself' method. It involves rejection of the illusory world on the one hand, and the development of Krishna consciousness on the other. Life within the sect is, therefore, a combination of asceticism and devotion.

The asceticism of Hare Krishna devotees is governed by four basic rules or prohibitions.

Rule one forbids all forms of gambling, various sports, and conversations not associated with the development of Krishna consciousness. Members of the sect do not readily engage in small talk!

Rule two forbids the use of alcohol, drugs, tobacco, tea and coffee. There is some relaxation in the case of drugs when they are prescribed by a doctor for medical purposes.

Rule three forbids illicit sex. This prohibition is surprising, however, in that it not only forbids pre-marital sex, as we should expect, but also sexual acts between married couples except for the procreation of children. Moreover, even in the case of married couples wishing to have children, intercourse must be undertaken only at the prescribed time each month and with the prior permission of the couple's spiritual superior. Before such intercourse, husband and wife are expected to prepare themselves by special devotions and must take care to do their best not to enjoy the act itself.

Rule four prescribes vegetarianism. Meat eaters, the movement believes, will be reborn either as animals, or as human beings destined to meet a violent end. The devotee is therefore expected to live almost entirely on a diet of milk, nuts, yoghurt and fruit. As they eat this, Krishna's energy is believed to flow through them.

As part of this ascetic life-style, designed to help the devotee to combat the illusions of the physical world and to encourage him in his growth towards Krishna consciousness, the male devotee must shave his head, every member must wear simple but distinctive clothing, and each is expected to exist on a maximum of six hours sleep a night. The head-shaving is for sexual reasons, for long hair is believed to be sexually attractive. The only part of the hair allowed to grow is the pigtail, with which, devotees believe, Krishna will pull them up to heaven.[17] The simple style of dress, a khirtan (shirt) and dhoti (loose trousers) for men and a sari for women, is also intended to play down physical attraction between the sexes. In recent years, however, there has been an interesting development in respect of dress, in that members are now sometimes permitted to wear wigs and conventional clothing when engaging in missionary work or selling their literature.

As well as the four prohibitions and the ascetic life-style, the Hare Krishna way of salvation requires a positive devotional life. This is focused on the familiar Hare Krishna chant, known as the mahamantra, which runs:

Hare Krishna, Hare Krishna,
Krishna Krishna, Hare Hare,
Hare Rama, Hara Rama,
Rama Rama, Hare Hare.

Prabhupada teaches that by chanting the holy name of

[17] Pat Means, op. cit., p. 148.

Krishna in this prescribed manner, his followers are taking the direct way to the Supreme Personality of Godhead.[18] Pure devotees are described as those whose minds are concerned only with this devotional activity. 'Twenty four hours daily they glorify the pastimes of the Supreme Lord. Their hearts and souls are constantly submerged in Krishna, and they take pleasure in discussing Him with other devotees.'[19] Realistically, however, Prabhupada points out, 'One travels throughout the universe before he is finally fortunate enough to meet a pure devotee.'[20]

A member who has not yet achieved such heights must persevere with his chanting. For example, a married man is expected to sit down morning and evening with his wife and children and, in addition to his own personal devotions at other times in the day, chant with them in the prescribed manner. He must decide for himself whether by doing this, carrying the additional burden of family life, he is achieving Krishna consciousness, which is his chief aim in life. If he is, then he may continue as a husband and father. Otherwise, instructs the Hare Krishna movement's founder, 'Family life should be abandoned.'[21] If he takes Prabhupada's advice and cuts his home ties, the devotee will of course be following the example his holy man has himself set.

The significance of the Hare Krishna chant is that it 'cleanses one's heart of all material dirt'.[22] It 'cleanses the accumulated dust of past karma from the mind'.[23] To encourage him in such important devotions, therefore, the devotee always wears a string of 108 beads, representing the 108 cowherdess lovers of Krishna, and in rosary-like fashion he uses his chant, once for each bead. As he faithfully engages in this duty, he is enveloped in a trance-like state and believes that at that time he is freed from the bondage of his body and the physical world and suspended in a state of pure spirit. The more faithfully he engages in his devotions, the longer his liberation lasts. As we have seen, his ultimate aim is complete deliverance from karma

[18] *Bhagavad-Gita As It Is*, p. 201.   [19] *Ibid.*, p. 167.   [20] *Ibid.*
[21] *Ibid.*, p. 212.   [22] *Ibid.*, p. 85.   [23] *Ibid.*, p. 211.

and its resulting endless chain of reincarnations and perfect union with Krishna in the movement's equivalent of heaven. Before he can begin to move towards this destiny, however, a man has to become a member of the Hare Krishna movement.

Levels of membership within the Hare Krishna movement

The steps that must be taken to become a fully-fledged member of the movement and to the higher levels of membership that may afterwards be attained, have been described fully by other writers.[24] Briefly, the procedures are as follows.

Before he is allowed to be initiated into the sect, the novice must prove himself by demonstrating his devotion to Krishna for a probationary period of about six months. During that time, he will live in a Hare Krishna commune, called a temple, and will be subject to the temple president, who will be responsible for mapping out every minute of his day. From the beginning the novice will need to learn that by joining the movement he is agreeing to allow a spiritual master to organize everything that he will do from that time onwards. There is no place for independence of thought or action within the sect. Loving Krishna involves obeying those the god has set over one.

After successfully passing through his probationary period, the novice is subjected to an elaborate initiation ceremony. Seven kinds of grain are thrown into a fire built in the middle of the room and butter is poured on top. After the prescribed chanting of the mahamantra, the initiate is given a new spiritual name in Sanskrit and receives the holy beads which he is expected to wear from then onwards for the rest of his life.

Six months later, the devotee undergoes another initiation known as his Brahminical initiation. At this stage, men are given a sacred thread to be worn over the left shoulder

[24] Ronald Enroth, *Youth, Brainwashing and the Extremist Cults* (Paternoster, 1977), pp. 23ff.

117

and across the chest and also a secret mantra which has to be chanted three times a day in addition to the regular use of the Hare Krishna chant. The devotee is now a full-fledged ordinary member of the Hare Krishna movement and need progress no further.

For the especially devoted, a further stage, that of the sannyasi, is possible. Like the traditional monk, the person makes his act of renunciation and takes life-long vows of poverty and celibacy. He also commits himself to a life of preaching and good works. Such a person is so highly regarded in the movement that others are expected to prostrate themselves before him.

At every level of membership, from that of the newest probationary recruit to that of the sannyasi holy man, life revolves around the temple-commune. Within this building all live under the strict surveillance of the temple president. There is complete segregation of the sexes in every aspect of temple life. Any idea of the equality of the sexes is quite foreign to the Hare Krishna movement. Men are regarded as superior to women, and women are expected to submit obediently to their menfolk. Temple music on bells, drums and finger cymbals is believed to provide 'transcendental sound vibrations' and thus encourage the life of devotion to Krishna.

Life in and around the temple follows a strictly regimented pattern. After rising at 3 a.m., devotees will take a cold shower and then apply tilaka to parts of their body. This is a paste made from clay flown in from India and is believed to sanctify and protect those who use it. As the devotee applies the paste to his forehead, his belly, his chest, his throat, between his collar bones, both arms, both sides of his waist, his upper and lower back, and to the top of his head, he says thirteen names of Krishna. After this, the devotee will probably engage in corporate and personal acts of devotion for two or three hours until, following breakfast and temple chores, he leaves the commune to engage in street work. Street work, the method of the movement's outreach, comprises activities like street chanting, group dancing, begging, and the sale of literature. The devotee returns to the temple in the middle of the day for lunch, and will then go out for perhaps another four or five hours of street work. Back again in the commune in the early evening, he will settle down to sleep at about 10 p.m., aware that he must rise again at 3 a.m. next day to begin the same routine all over again.

Within the temple, the president's authority is unchallenged. He himself answers only to his spiritual master. Subject to that over-all authority, the temple president controls the life of all those attached to the temple. He decides which tasks each is to do for the general upkeep of the temple, he arranges their marriages, he acts as their spiritual counsellor, and where necessary he settles disputes between them. As Krishna's local representative he expects obedience from devotees, and usually gets it.

For all devotees alike, however, no matter how high or low their personal status may be within the sect, the chief aim is the growth of Krishna consciousness. This means that they are concerned, not only with their own spiritual development, but also with the spread of Krishna consciousness to those outside the movement. Every devotee regards himself, therefore, as an ambassador for Krishna and this has very practical implications on his daily timetable. On average he will spend about six hours chanting in his private and corporate devotions, the Hare Krishna mahamantra being chanted at least 1,728 times, and will spend another six hours or more in street work. The street work, as we have seen, includes chanting, begging, dancing, and selling the sect's literature.

It is important to remember that members regard street chanting as perhaps the most effective method of spreading their ideas and winning converts. They believe that, as they chant, their onlookers are impressed and often stunned by the power and purity of chanting the holy name of Krishna and become receptive to their message. The people thus contacted who show further interest are encouraged to link up with the local temple-commune and thus the whole process of leading people into full membership, described earlier, is put into operation. Using such methods, the movement has won perhaps a thousand converts since it began work in Britain in 1969.

The Hare Krishna movement and Christianity

Because of their desire to extend their work in Britain, Hare
Krishna devotees sometimes suggest that there are few
basic differences between themselves and Christians. They
are doing for Krishna what Christians claim to be doing
for Christ. Are not the differences simply those of terminology? It is of course true that their particular brand of
Hinduism comes closer to Christianity than do some other
forms of that religion. Like Christians, Hare Krishna devotees believe that God is personal and that man's salvation
is to be understood in terms of a personal relationship with
God. It needs to be understood, however, that despite the
similarities in some areas of belief and practice, the Hare
Krishna movement is very definitely a Hindu sect and that
what it is trying to do is to expand its particular brand of
Hinduism. Because of that, Christians will wish to take
careful note of the differences, though treating Hare Krishna devotees with respect and recognizing their sincerity
and zeal in the cause which they have embraced.

In the first place, Christians will wish to point out that,
although acknowledging the supremacy of one god, Krishna, the Hare Krishna movement is still essentially poly-
theistic in that it regards Krishna as the chief god among
many. A quick glance through Prabhupada's commentary
on the *Bhagavad-Gita* reveals that he acknowledges the galaxy of the Hindu gods, among whom he refers particularly
to Agni the god of fire, Brahma the chief among the demi-
gods, Indra the king of the heavenly planets, Laksmi the
goddess of fortune, Manu the administrative demigod who
is the father of mankind, Shiva the god of destruction, and
Vivasvan the sun god. In contrast, Christians are fully
committed monotheists, for even though we recognize a
trinity within the Godhead, the Father, the Son and the
Holy Spirit are not *three gods* but *one God*.

The respective attitudes of the Hare Krishna movement
and Christianity to the physical world also differ widely.
As we have seen, Prabhupada and his disciples follow the
traditional Hindu doctrine of maya, believing that the material world is an illusion. They go on to state that only by

accepting it as illusory will the individual find his true self in Krishna consciousness. In contrast, though recognizing that 'Here we have no continuing city' and looking for the return of Christ when the present world .will pass away, Christians believe that there is nothing illusory or essentially evil about the material world in itself, for God created it. Christians do not therefore wish to reject the world's reality but wish to work in it to God's glory, their views being governed by the belief that 'the Word became flesh'.

Again, though Christians would wish to welcome the Hare Krishna belief in the continuance of the human personality beyond this life (in contrast with that Hindu tradition which looks for the individual's complete absorption and thus disappearance within ultimate reality), they could not support the accompanying Hare Krishna beliefs about karma and reincarnation. Christians believe that life on earth here and now is man's one probationary time, that 'Now is the day of salvation', that after death comes judgment. Then man's final destiny will be decided once and for all. Christians do not believe, therefore, that the individual soul's future consists of a series of reincarnations (perhaps in animal, perhaps in human, form) until liberation is finally achieved. Rather, they look to Christ for eternal life, which begins here and now for the believer, but which continues by the sure and certain hope of resurrection to a new body suited to a new environment in heaven, as set out clearly by Paul in 1 Corinthians 15.

Again, whereas this sect's devotees believe that salvation is achieved by a person's ceaseless devotional activities, Christians believe that salvation is a gift of God, earned by Christ, offered by grace, and to be accepted individually by faith.

Christians will have mixed feelings about the movement's four rules. Though some would view with sympathy much of what the Hare Krishna movement is demanding of its members, all Christians would ask for freedom of conscience to make their own decisions. They would also wish to challenge in the strongest possible way the rule relating to sex. If, as Christians believe, sex is a gift of God to be shared between partners within a loving marriage relationship, they cannot possibly allow someone outside that relationship to dictate to them when and for what purpose and with whom sexual intercourse is to take place.

In fact, Christians would wish to take the strongest possible exception to almost everything that the Hare Krishna movement has to say about marriage and family life. Quite apart from the strange attitude to the sex act itself, and the instruction that devotees must make an effort not to enjoy it, there is the clear statement by the movement's founder that if a devotee's family life is not conducive to his growth in Krishna consciousness he is at liberty to retire from it. Those who believe that in Christian marriage they are pledging themselves to a life-long union cannot accept this view. Christians, like others, are free to remain unmarried and celibate, and some of them, believing this to be God's call to them, follow this path. But that is very different from the view that the marriage partner may be dropped and the devotee may, almost casually it seems, retire from marriage for what he regards as his own spiritual improvement. Christians would wish to say that it is as they face their difficulties, including those within their own family circle, with the strength God gives them, so they grow in grace.

This strange attitude to possible problems in family life highlights one other factor that needs to be noted in considering the fundamental differences between the Hare Krishna movement and Christianity. It is stated succinctly by William Petersen,[25] who shows that the Hare Krishna movement evades all the important issues. 'The key problems are not solved but dissolved . . . Everything that you need to be saved from is declared to be an illusion'. In contrast, the Christian faith recognizes the reality of the fallen world, the fact of sinful human nature, and all the warped attitudes found within society as a result. Then it goes on to show Christians what God has done in Christ to put it right.

Although the Hare Krishna movement recognizes that the heart needs to be cleansed, it confines the problem to 'material dirt' (which presumably means undue attachment

[25] William Petersen, *Those Curious New Cults*, p. 172.

to the illusory world) and offers as the solution the constant chanting of the mahamantra. But the Christian faith is much more realistic, both in its assessment of the problem and in its provision of the solution. Jeremiah makes the diagnosis, 'The heart is the most deceitful of all things, desperately sick.'[26] Jesus illustrated the point aptly when he said, 'Wicked thoughts, murder, adultery, fornication, theft, perjury, slander – these all proceed from the heart; and these are the things that defile a man.'[27] John states the solution and so takes us to the heart of the Christian gospel: 'Should anyone commit a sin, we have one to plead our cause with the Father, Jesus Christ, and he is just. He is himself the remedy for the defilement of our sins, not our sins only but the sins of all the world.'[28] Because Christians believe *this* gospel, they have no alternative than to reject the inadequate solution to man's basic need offered by Prabhupada and his Hare Krishna movement.

Summary of main differences

Hare Krishna	Christianity
God	
Among the Hindu galaxy of gods, Krishna reigns supreme.	There is one God, yet within the unity of the Godhead there are three divine Persons, Father, Son and Holy Spirit.
Reality	
The only reality is spiritual reality. The material world and all associated with it is an illusion.	God is concerned about the whole material world, which he created, and into which he sent his Son as an incarnate being.
Future life	
Following the Hindu tradition, the Hare	The Bible teaches that after this life all will be

[26] Jeremiah 17:9.   [27] Matthew 15:19–20.   [28] 1 John 2:1–2.

Krishna movement believes in reincarnation, an endless cycle of birth, death and rebirth, the form of any one reincarnation being determined by behaviour in the former existence.

judged on the basis of their relationship with God through Jesus Christ. Their eternal destiny will then be decided.

Salvation

Salvation comes through union with Krishna through the development of Krishna consciousness and by the observance of rules governing every aspect of life.

By appropriating by faith all that Christ has done on our behalf, we are saved from sin and given new life in Christ. 'There is no salvation in anyone else at all, for there is no other name under heaven granted to men, by which we may receive salvation' (Acts 4:12).

8. Scientology

The founder of Scientology, L. Ron Hubbard, claims that he derived the sect's name from the Latin *scio*, which he translates as 'knowing in the fullest meaning of the word', and the Greek *logos*, which he renders 'to study'.[1] Scientology is said to provide answers to such fundamental questions as 'Who am I?', 'Where do I come from?', 'What is death?', and 'Is there a life hereafter?' It claims to be a search for ultimate truth leading to absolute freedom. The person who follows the sect's processes and reaches this goal of truth and freedom is described as 'clear', whilst the rest of us remain as 'pre-clears'.

Describing itself as 'an applied religious philosophy of life and a body of knowledge concerning man and his relationship to the Universe and to his fellows',[2] Scientology claims to possess what it calls 'a technology for spiritual recovery and the increase of individual ability'.[3] Scientologists assert that, when this technology is applied, it is 'capable uniformly of raising or recovering the spiritual condition of an individual to a more desirable level, either to make the less able more able or to make the able more able'.[4] They describe their sect as 'the most vital and widespread self-betterment movement on earth today' and as 'man's most advanced school of the Mind'.[5] Hubbard him-

---

[1] L. Ron Hubbard, *The Fundamentals of Thought* (The Church of Scientology, 1956), p. 12.
[2] *Report to Members of Parliament on Scientology.*
[3] *The Character of Scientology.*   [4] *Ibid.*, p. 13.
[5] *Scientology*, Vol. 1 No. 1, pp. 4 and 11.

self has claimed, 'It can and does change behaviour and intelligence and it can and does assist people to study life'.[6] The aim of Scientology is 'to make man into a higher being'.[7]

According to the sect's publications, there are two distinct parts to Scientology: its philosophy and its technology. Its philosophy 'lays down the creeds and codes of the Church (and) contains the beliefs, the record of research, and the findings'.[8] The technology applies these findings to individuals, enabling them to become better communicators and better at handling problems, confronting failures, and being more successful.[9] Although it is this 'technology' (so called) which attracts attention to the movement, Scientology's chief claim is in the realm of philosophy and religion. It stresses that it is a church which is committed to an applied philosophy leading its adherents in a search for that truth and freedom through the attainment of which they become better people.

Although Scientologists claim a world-membership of some 15,000,000, others say they number no more than about 3,000,000. There may be about 200,000 British Scientologists. The sect operates from Saint Hill Manor, East Grinstead, Sussex, which Hubbard bought from the Maharajah of Jaipur in 1959. The real focus of power is now to be found, however, on Sea Org, a well-equipped trio of ships on the high seas, where Hubbard has lived ever since he was refused entry to Britain.

The sect does not seem to hit the headlines as often now as it did in the 1960s and early 1970s, when it was engaged in a series of lawsuits with various public figures, including the then Minister of Health and some members of parliament, and with a number of journalists, authors and publishers. By and large, however, Scientology appears to be working away more quietly and there is reason to believe that its membership continues to grow steadily.

But what is known about its founder? What are the sect's

---

[6] *The Fundamentals of Thought*, p. 12.   [7] *Scientology*, Vol.1 No.1, p. 20.
[8] Leaflet by the Public Relations Bureau of the Church of Scientology.
[9] *Ibid.*

beliefs? How does it operate? What relation does it bear to religion in general and Christianity in particular? And what is its attraction? These are the questions to which we must now address ourselves.

The founder of Scientology

Lafayette Ronald Hubbard was born at Tilden, Nebraska, USA on 13 March 1911 to an American naval commander, H. R. Hubbard, and his wife, Dora May. Because his father's career necessitated constant travel, Ron (as he is known throughout the sect) spent his early years in the care of his grandfather on a cattle ranch in Montana. In adolescence, however, he rejoined his parents, travelling with them to the Far East. There he developed an interest in the nature of man and began studying Asian religions. Later he was to travel extensively, and claims that his many contacts with medicine men in Manchuria, among the Sioux Indians, with the Shamans of North Borneo, with members of various cults in Los Angeles, and with exponents of modern psychology, mysticism and spiritualism, helped form the background against which he formulated his own philosophical system.[10]

Scientologists often claim that their founder is a man of academic distinction and expertise, though there is no hard evidence to support such assertions. What is not in doubt, however, is that all through the 1930s Hubbard was writing to earn a living. His repertoire included westerns, science fiction and adventure stories, as well as film scripts.

Hubbard served in the United States navy during the Second World War and is said to draw a disability pension, though it is not clear whether he was wounded in active service or developed a pensionable illness. He himself claims that he was at death's door when discharged from the navy but that by 1949 he had recovered sufficiently to have been pronounced physically fit.[11]

The beginnings of what we now call Scientology began

---

[10] *The Evolution of a Science*, pp. 14ff.

[11] *Scientology*, Vol.1 No.1, p. 7.

in 1950 with the publication of Hubbard's book, *Dianetics: The Modern Science of Mental Health*, which his followers still regard as 'a major breakthrough in the history of Man'.[12] A psychologist has described how Dianetics quickly became a fad, especially among students and Hollywood film stars.[13] It dealt with what Hubbard called 'the reactive mind', which corresponds roughly with what others call the unconscious or the subconscious. Later it was to be followed by Scientology, dealing with 'the thetan', which corresponds partly with what Christians know as the spirit. Scientology thus evolved from Dianetics, attempting to give what was essentially a book of psychological techniques a philosophical basis.

As with Mary Baker Eddy and her Christian Science, Hubbard has always maintained that he did not create Scientology but merely discovered it. He claims that it was the perfect fulfilment of what all the followers of other religions had been searching for through the centuries of religious history. Because of this claim, Scientologists are able to regard the truths found in Hinduism, Buddhism, Taoism, Judaism, Christianity and various western philosophers as a preparation for that supreme truth discovered and proclaimed by Hubbard.

> Scientology has accomplished the goal of religion expressed in all man's written history, the freeing of the soul by wisdom. It is a far more intellectual religion than that known to the West as late as 1950.[14]

Others are less convinced by Hubbard's claims, for what he seems to have done is to select widely from whatever writings appealed to him, to re-write those selected extracts in his own peculiar, pseudo-psychological jargon, and then to incorporate this in his own system. By its very nature, therefore, Scientology is syncretistic.

The opponents of Scientology have often alleged that Hubbard has become a very rich man by means of its

---

[12] *Ibid.*   [13] Dr Christopher Evans in *The Observer*, 11 August 1968.
[14] *The Character of Scientology*, p. 8.

expensive courses, but Scientologists always retort that their founder was a very rich man before 1954 and that, if anything, the church owes him money. Until the recent change of mind by the British government, he and other foreign scientologists were refused entry to Britain. Hubbard now appears to spend most of his time sailing the high seas in his ship Sea Org, which is in constant touch with East Grinstead by means of highly sophisticated radio equipment.

The beliefs of Scientology

As noted earlier, Scientology is in fact a combination of Dianetics and Scientology. The former is described by Scientologists as a study of the exact anatomy of the human mind, and the latter as a study of that which animates the mind. Less flatteringly, others have asserted that whereas Dianetics is a poor copy of psycho-analysis, Scientology stems directly from Hubbard's creative ability as a writer of science fiction. Readers will need to consult longer books for a fuller treatment of the sect's beliefs. All that is attempted here is an outline of some of Scientology's key ideas.

The thetan

According to Hubbard, the thetan is man's spirit or essential being. Without quoting any supporting evidence, he makes the astonishing claim that he has proved scientifically 'that the thing which is the person, the personality, is separable from the body and mind at will' without causing death or derangement.[15] He says that although the thetan is normally resident in the skull, it is one of the goals of Scientology to exteriorize it in such a way that it is outside but near the body, knowingly controlling it.

Dramatic claims are made about the thetan's power. It can remould the body, increasing or reducing its weight and height and changing its appearance,[16] it can manufac-

---

[15] *The Fundamentals of Thought*, p. 58.
[16] L. Ron Hubbard, *A History of Man*, p. 10.

ture a body or a facsimile of one,[17] it can emit enough electricity to give someone a nasty shock or a fatal injury,[18] and it can move material objects and travel at high speeds. It is not bound by atmosphere or temperature. Hubbard warns his followers not to show off to prove the thetan's power by knocking off hats at fifty yards distance or by reading books a couple of countries away.[19]

Hubbard states that the thetan cannot die and is constantly being reincarnated either on earth or on some other planet. Although each individual has experienced many lives in different bodies, the same theta being has been common to them all.[20] Hubbard expects these ideas to be accepted literally, for, he explains, 'This is a cold-blooded and factual account of your last sixty trillion years.'[21]

He maintains that the thetan joins its designated body immediately prior to its birth. Moreover, thetans are not always as good as they ought to be, and sometimes there is even a dispute over 'housing'. Two thetans have been known to attempt to join the same body and have had to fight it out.[22] At death the thetan leaves the body and goes to the 'between-lives' area, where, after reporting in, it is given a strong 'forgetter implant' before being shot down to join another body just before that body is born. The report area for most thetans is Mars, though some women, Hubbard explains, have to make do with stations elsewhere in the solar system.[23]

After noting all this, readers may need little persuading that Hubbard is, according to the unconscious irony of one of the sect's publications, 'still one of the better known science fiction writers'.[24]

The mind

Dianetics, claimed as 'a study of the exact anatomy of the human mind', points the way to total freedom. Its basic idea is that the dynamic principle of existence is the urge to survive. The brain, which Hubbard describes as a com-

[17] Ibid.   [18] Ibid., p. 32.   [19] Ibid., p. 34.
[20] Ibid., p. 13.   [21] Ibid., p. 1.   [22] Ibid., p. 13.
[23] Ibid., p. 50.   [24] Scientology, Vol.1 No.1, p. 7.

puter which solves problems relating to survival, acts upon its own best-conceived but personally viewpointed plan for survival. He also discusses the 'optimum brain', which he defines as the brain 'unaberrated', concluding that this is man's basic personality which is good.[25] But therein lies the problem. If man is basically good, how does he become evil?

According to Hubbard, the problem lies, not in man himself, but in the exterior world. How, then, does this exterior world lead to an individual's interior aberrations? The philosophy of Scientology is Hubbard's explanation and its technology its cure.

Returning to his theory of the optimum or unaberrated brain, Hubbard explains that this brain is intrinsically accurate, like a perfect computer, a quality essential in an organ dedicated to the tasks of computing a life-and-death matter like survival. He labels this optimum or unaberrated brain the analytical mind and says it is this which distinguishes human beings from the rest of the animals.[26]

Against this background, Hubbard expounds his theory of evil, which to him means simply irrational behaviour. In language not far removed from that of the modern psychology which he claims to have rejected, he states that every perception observed in a lifetime is stored in the human memory bank. Such memories, which include painful and unpleasant memories, are 'filed by time'. 'They have an age and emotional label, and a precise and exhaustive record of everything perceived by organic sensation.'[27] Now a perfect computer such as the human brain ought to be capable of handling anything fed into it. What, then, goes wrong in the human mind? How does it become aberrated? The villain in the piece turns out to be what Hubbard calls the reactive mind, which he defines as a 'stimulus-response' mind.[28] Linked to this is Hubbard's theory of engrams,[29] that is, energy pictures made during a period of physical pain 'when the analyzer is out of circuit

[25] *The Evolution of a Science*, pp. 31f.
[26] *Ibid*, pp. 47f.   [27] *Ibid.*, p. 54.   [28] *Ibid.*, p. 62.
[29] 'Engrams' is a term used in neurophysiology denoting a memory trace.

131

and the organism experiences something it conceives to be or which is contrary to survival'.[30]

It is easier to understand Hubbard's theory of engrams by looking at one of his own examples. Mary (aged two) is attacked by a dog, knocked to the ground and bitten. The contents of the engram experience are anaten (*i.e.* unconsciousness), Mary's age, and all that she then sees, smells, feels and hears. The sum total of this unpleasant experience is, as it were, filed away in the human memory bank and Mary forgets the incident. When she is twelve, however, she has another similar experience which re-stimulates the engram. As a result, whenever she hears a dog bark she gets a headache![31]

Although this may be very interesting, Hubbard is not really telling us anything new. Psychologists speak in similar language. The mind of man is like an island, the conscious part being the small piece above the surface and the unconscious or subconscious being the greater part below the surface which goes down to the bed of the ocean. The unconscious is the storehouse of memories and the seat of impulses, drives and neuroses. The unconscious 'registers' all the experiences, ideas and reactions of the individual. Repression is the process by which a complex (that is, a constellation of ideas with a strong emotional overtone) becomes involuntarily buried in the unconscious. Psychiatrists quote case histories of patients in whom repressions have led to bad repercussions on outlook and behaviour and where some form of psychotherapy has been necessary to bring the causes of the disturbance 'into the open'.

Now all of this was known long before Hubbard wrote about 'the exact anatomy of the human mind'. What he seems to have done is to take up some of the ideas of psychology, to have dressed them up in certain 'Hubbardisms' like 'analytical mind', 'reactive mind' and 'anaten', to have combined these with ideas from other sources, and to have put forward the whole conglomeration as first Dianetics and later Scientology. This is certainly

---

[30] *The Evolution of a Science*, p. 63.   [31] *Ibid.*, pp. 65f.

not the major breakthrough in the history of man that Scientologists claim for Hubbard's work. Dr Christopher Evans' description of it as 'ill-considered, jargon-riddled schoolboy psychology' seems nearer the mark.[32]

The Eight Dynamics
As we have seen, Hubbard regarded the urge to survive as the fundamental principle of existence. He subdivided this urge into a number of drives or impulses of life, at first four in Dianetics and later four more in Scientology. He called them dynamics. The eight are as follows:

1. The Self-Dynamic – the urge towards existence as an individual, conscious of one's personal identity.
2. The Sex-Dynamic – the urge towards existence as a sexual or bisexual activity, including the sex act itself and the family unit.
3. The Group-Dynamic – the urge towards existence in groups, such as schools, towns, nations.
4. The Mankind-Dynamic – the urge towards existence of the human race as a whole.
5. The Animal-Dynamic – the urge towards all living things, whether vegetable or animal.
6. The Universe-Dynamic – the urge towards existence as the physical universe.
7. The Spiritual-Dynamic – the urge towards existence *as* or *of* spirits.
8. The God-Dynamic – the urge towards existence as infinity.

Among Scientologists, these eight dynamics are used as a standard against which to measure a person's abilities and shortcomings.

As a person expands in Scientology he is able to expand outwards through these dynamics to the eighth – God or infinity. . . . It is not a ladder upwards! Rather a series of concentric circles, with the person being inside

[32] *The Observer*, 11 August 1968.

the first circle, and from there expanding outwards across all the others.[33]

Hubbard himself illustrates their usage.

One discovers that a baby at birth is not perceptive beyond the First Dynamic, but as the child grows and interests extend it can be seen to embrace other dynamics. As a further example of use, a person who is incapable of operating on the Third Dynamic is incapable at once of being a part of a team and so might be said to be incapable of a social existence.[34]

Again, one may comment that there is nothing very new about this. Classification of drives, impulses, instincts or propensities were being made long before Hubbard discovered Dianetics or Scientology. The psychologist McDougall made the classification of human instincts or propensities the foundation of his psychology, listing eighteen propensities and stating that these 'driving forces' were 'the very foundation of all mental life'.[35] One does not need to be a Scientologist (or a psychologist) to be aware of the fact that at first a baby is completely bound up in himself, having little consciousness of any being outside himself. It is also obvious to all that the person who has no urge towards what Hubbard calls the Group-Dynamic will not be very gregarious. Those who are not Scientologists will find it difficult to see such 'truths' as part of Hubbard's great breakthrough, because they have accepted such 'truths' all along!

For the Christian, the seventh and eighth dynamics are interesting, in the light of Scientology's claim to be a religion. The seventh dynamic requires a person not only to recognize that there is a spiritual part of his own nature, but also that this is a separate entity, the thetan, which has

---

[33] A leading British Scientologist explained this in a personal letter to the author, 29 October 1969.

[34] *The Fundamentals of Thought*, p. 41.

[35] According to R. H. Thouless in *General and Social Psychology*.

existed for trillions of years and will continue to be reincarnated in the years to come. Moreover, it can be encouraged by means of Scientology processing to float away from its body. Although Hubbard's list closes with the God-Dynamic, there is little else about God in Scientology. One might be tempted to say that God has been added as an afterthought, but that is a subject to which we must return shortly.

The methods of Scientology

After an initial stimulation of interest, perhaps through picking up a piece of the sect's literature, or following conversation with a Scientologist, or after undergoing a free personality test at one of the movement's centres, the contact will be persuaded to undertake an Auditor's Course, where he will learn about 'the anatomy of the human mind' and 'will gain practical experience in handling it in actual auditing sessions'.[36] This will lead in turn to more advanced courses, either at a 'local academy', or, for the most advanced courses, at Saint Hill Manor, East Grinstead, site of the Hubbard College of Scientology. Scientologists willingly spend hundreds of pounds on such courses, believing they are the stepping-stones to 'the incredibly high state of Clear', that is, total mental and spiritual freedom.

Those who submit to such processing are promised very practical results.

Scientology processing among other things can improve the intelligence quotient of an individual, his ability or desire to communicate, his social attitudes, his capability and domestic harmony, his fertility, his artistic creativity, his reaction time and his health.[37]

In fact, 'The progress of tendencies, neuroses, habits, and deteriorating activities can be halted by Scientology or their occurrence can be prevented.'[38]

[36] *Scientology*, Vol.1 No.1, p. 17.
[37] *The Fundamentals of Thought*, p. 99.   [38] *Ibid.*

All that these appear to be is a rather second-class type of psycho-analysis. The student sits in front of an E-Meter, which is described by Scientologists as a twentieth-century confessional aid but which is really a rather unsophisticated kind of lie detector. His partner, the 'auditor', asks the student a series of questions aimed at probing into what most people, though not Scientologists, would call his unconscious. During this question-and-answer session, the pre-clear holds an electrode in each hand. The electrical impulses registered by the E-Meter are said to indicate the presence of engrams in his reactive mind. As these engrams are brought to light, the pre-clear achieves his grade of release and may then proceed to the next course.

Scientology and psychiatry

By now it will have become obvious to most readers that Scientology is attempting to deal with a field usually associated with psychiatrists and psychiatric treatment. Indeed, some of the sect's techniques are very similar to those used by some psychiatrists, and it is hard to avoid the conclusion that in dealing with engrams Scientologists are seeking to deal with what the rest of us usually call the unconscious. Though Scientologists make it clear that they never knowingly deal with those suffering from mental illness, there is obviously an area here that inevitably leads to some overlap. What, then, is the attitude of Scientology to psychiatry? In a phrase, the answer is unrelenting hostility.

Scientology publications often contain bitter attacks directed towards psychiatrists. The hostility came to a head in 1969 when leading British Scientologists tried to get themselves elected to key positions within the executive of the National Association for Mental Health, following the infiltration of the Association by more than two hundred Scientologists. The Association responded by expelling these Scientologists from membership. There then followed a legal wrangle (carefully documented by C. H. Rolph in *Believe What You Like*), the outcome of which was that the Association's right to expel Scientologists from membership

136

was upheld.

Three main reasons are given by Scientologists for their attacks upon psychiatry. They claim that some forms of psychiatric treatment, electroplexy and leucotomy in particular, are inhuman and ought to be stopped. They believe that there are political motives behind much of what is done in the name of psychiatry, maintaining that there is an international 'psychiatric front group' which attempts to control governments and thus bring whole nations into servitude. They also assert that psychiatry is fundamentally opposed to every great truth that religion counts dear. Because such charges are so serious, it is necessary to look at them in a little more detail.

Regarding the first claim, that some forms of psychiatric treatment are inhuman, it needs to be remembered that no-one, least of all the psychiatrists themselves, would claim that mistakes have never been made, though this was probably more common in the early days of psychiatry than it is today. But Scientologists exaggerate the dangers and disasters. On the opposite side, thousands of people could testify that their mental health has improved dramatically after such treatment.

Concerning the second claim, about the unworthy political motives behind psychiatry, there is no doubt that in some countries on some occasions psychiatrists (along with scientists, historians, and even the clergy) have been used in such ways. The history of Nazi Germany and more recent occurrences in certain other totalitarian states provide evidence. On the other hand, the wild charge that all psychiatrists are part of an incredible plan for world domination is so absurd that it scarcely deserves to be treated seriously. From my own past experience as a chaplain in a psychiatric hospital I would find the whole idea laughable, were it not for the effect that such a charge could have upon a mentally ill person who needs treatment in a psychiatric hospital.

The third charge, that psychiatry is a direct attack upon all religious truth, is constantly reiterated in Scientology literature. 'All attacks on Scientology churches stem from psychiatric circles', is a typical example from the magazine

Freedom. Anyone who has taken the trouble to read that magazine, however, and who has but a nodding acquaintance with psychiatry, will quickly conclude that there are much more likely grounds for opposition. The following is a typical example.

> There are no insane. There are only the physically ill. 'Insanity' is a non-existent malady invented to mystify and horrify the public. Any person who looks or acts irrational is either: (a) physically ill and in suppressed pain and agony, (b) is in terror at being declared 'insane' . . . There is no illness called 'insanity'. It is a symptom of other recognisable, curable ills.

The alleged conflict between religion and psychiatry was portrayed in a particularly vicious cartoon in the Scientology magazine *International Freedom*. A huge figure of death wielding a scythe labelled 'Psychiatry' was shown addressing Christ on the cross with the words, 'Down you come. I'm looking after things now. Your kind are no longer needed.' The same paper claims that psychiatry ridicules the Bible and its teaching and advocates promiscuous sexual behaviour and perversion.

Now of course it is true that it would be possible to point to a number of prominent psychiatrists who have denied the existence of God, rejected the teachings of Christianity, or decried the Christian ethic. Similarly, it would not be difficult to find scientists, agriculturalists, or even philatelists, who have adopted the same kind of stance, but we would not then go on to argue that science, agriculture or stamp-collecting as such were irreligious. Among all walks of life and every type of profession there are believers and unbelievers, and certainly there are many psychiatrists who are practising Christians.

One of the best-known Christian psychiatrists in this country is Dr Stafford-Clark. Recognizing that some ardent disciples of materialistic psychology have made anti-religious claims, but showing how the patient, 'groping beyond himself for the final answer, cannot get it from the analyst', Dr Stafford-Clark asks in his book *Psychiatry Today*,

Where then can a man turn? If full self-awareness and self-realization are not by themselves enough, what is? As a psychiatrist I know of no answer to this question: as a man I can only say with all humility that I believe in God.

The religion of Scientology

Is Scientology a religion? The answer is determined by which definition of religion is used. One definition describes religion as a 'system of faith and worship; human recognition of superhuman controlling power and especially of a personal God entitled to obedience'.[39] Another states that religion is 'man's attempt to supplement his felt insufficiency by allying himself with a higher order of being which he believes is manifest in the world and which can be brought into sympathetic relationship with himself, if rightly approached'.[40] Using the first definition, we may well conclude that Scientology is not a religion, for ideas of a personal God and worship are not an integral part of the system. Using the second definition, however, it might be felt that Scientology is a religion.

Scientologists themselves certainly claim that their movement is a religion, 'an applied religious philosophy'. Mary Sue Hubbard, the founder's third wife, maintains,

Scientology is a religion in the oldest sense of the word, a study of wisdom. Scientology is a study of man as a spirit, in his relationship to life and the physical universe. It is non-denominational. By that it is meant that Scientology is open to people of all religions and beliefs and in no way tries to persuade a person from his religion, but assists him better to understand that he is a spiritual being.[41]

Leaving aside the assertion that the origins of religion

[39] Concise Oxford Dictionary.
[40] E. S. Waterhouse, The Philosophical Approach to Religion (Epworth, 1964), p. 24.   [41] Freedom, No. 13

are to be found in the search for wisdom, which anthropologists as well as Christians would challenge, it is important to notice what Mrs Hubbard omits. There is no mention of God and therefore no mention of any kind of relationship between human beings and a divine Being. Again, there is no mention of prayer or worship. These are not accidental omissions. A person can be a good Scientologist without believing in God and, therefore, without possessing any sense of the need to worship him, or to pray to him, or to be in a right relationship with him.

It would seem reasonable to assume that Scientologists who do believe in God believed in him before becoming Scientologists. Similarly, those who worship and pray were involved in such activities before joining the sect and have carried their earlier practices over into Scientology. It is not surprising to find, therefore, that one member finds no conflict between the Jewish faith into which she was born and her Scientology to which she was converted, and that another prominent Scientologist still regards himself as a member of the Church of England.

Scientologists would claim, however, that what all the religions of the world have been feeling after for centuries has now been revealed in its fullness through the work of Ron Hubbard. 'Scientology has accomplished the goal of religion expressed in all man's written history, the freeing of the soul by wisdom.'[42] Some go further, implying that Scientology has superseded other religions. So one writer claims that other religions tried to answer questions about man's origin and destiny but 'their answers have varied through the ages and race to race and this variation alone is the stumbling block which brings disbelief into faiths. Old religions fade because people do not find answers to the above questions real . . . The decline of Christianity is marked by modern cynicism about a hell where one burns for an eternity and a Heaven where one plays a harp for ever.' On the other hand, in Scientology 'the superstition has been subtracted from spiritual studies'.[43]

Scientology has its own creed, but readers will not find

[42] *The Character of Scientology*, p. 8.   [43] *Scientology*, Vol.1 No.1, p. 13.

it a clear doctrinal statement comparable to the creeds of mainstream Christianity. After all, 'Scientology does not include within it cold and musty data. It answers the questions of philosophy and religion with scientific truths.'[44] More than half the creed of Scientology is a statement of human rights to which very few civilized people would take exception. From the religious point of view, the most significant sections of the creed appear in the second half. One of these reads,

And we of the Church believe:
That man is basically good.
That he is seeking to survive.
That his survival depends upon himself and upon his fellows, and his attainment of brotherhood with the Universe.

The other states,

And we of the Church believe:
That the spirit can be saved and
That the spirit alone may save or heal the body.

Here we have four positive statements, showing that Scientologists believe in (a) the essential goodness of man, (b) human survival, (c) the need of salvation for the spirit, and (d) the ability of the spirit to save and heal the body. This is the nearest one gets to a doctrine of salvation. It will not have escaped the reader's notice that it is largely salvation by self-effort. There is no doctrine of a Saviour. Even more surprisingly, except by implication the creed does not state the need to believe in God.

In fairness to the sect's founder, it must be pointed out that Hubbard has declared his own belief in the existence of a Supreme Being.

No culture in the history of the world (he has stated), save the thoroughly depraved and expiring ones, has

[44] *Ibid.*, p. 25.

failed to affirm the existence of a Supreme Being. It is an empirical observation that men without a strong and lasting faith in a Supreme Being are less capable, less ethical, and less valuable to themselves and society . . . A man without an abiding faith is . . . more of a thing than a man.[45]

It should be noted also that the last of Hubbard's eight dynamics is the God-Dynamic, which is explained as 'survival through a Supreme Being, or more exactly, Infinity'.[46] As stated earlier, however, although members of the sect believe in God, such belief does not seem to be an integral part of Scientology. Nevertheless, the sect was registered as The Church of Scientology of California on 19 May 1954, its stated aim being, 'To establish a religious fellowship and association for the research into the spirit and human soul, and the use and dissemination of its findings'.[47]

Scientology and Christianity

Even if we recognize Scientology as a religion, however, there can be no doubt that in certain very important aspects Scientology and Christianity not only differ but are diametrically opposed.

Scientologists have published a sixty-four page booklet called *Scientology and the Bible*, which claims to be 'A Manifest Paralleling of the Discoveries of Scientology by L. Ron Hubbard with the Holy Scriptures'. Its aim seems to be that of showing that there is no essential difference between the teachings of the movement's founder and the teachings of the Bible. Anyone looking for a serious-minded attempt to relate the two will be disappointed. Half the booklet makes sense – the right-hand column of each page which quotes the Bible, the early church fathers and the historic Christian creeds. The other half, the left-hand columns, quoting Hubbard's writings, is even more absurd read alongside the Bible than when it is seen in isolation. One

[45] *The Science of Survival*, p. 98.   [46] *Scientology*, Vol.1 No.1, p. 27.
[47] *Report to Members of Parliament on Scientology*.

or two examples will demonstrate the point.

Proverbs 21:2, 'Every way of a man is right in his own eyes: but the Lord pondereth the heart', is put alongside 'The value of a datum or a field of data is modified by the viewpoint of the observer'. John 15:13, 'Greater love hath no man than this, that a man lay down his life for his friends', is explained by 'Never desert a comrade in trouble'. John 10:28, 'I give unto them eternal life; and they shall never perish, neither shall any man pluck them out of my hand', is unbelievably equated with 'Life is basically a static', whilst Psalm 40:2, 'He brought me up also out of a horrible pit, out of the miry clay, and set my feet upon a rock, and established my goings', is supposed to mean the same thing as, 'An actuality can exist for one individually, but when it is agreed with by others it can then be said to be a reality.'

All of this makes sad reading, especially as it comes from a movement which claims, among other things, to be able to improve its adherents' ability to communicate! To the non-Scientologist most of Hubbard's statements quoted above are meaningless, and it is difficult to see how any intelligent person, whatever his religious commitment, can honestly believe that they have anything in common with the scriptural passages they accompany.

When we move on to compare some of the basic ideas of Scientology with some of the key doctrines of the Christian faith, we quickly see that the two have little or nothing in common. In particular, it is clear that in at least four vital areas Christianity and Scientology are either diametrically opposed or have no common ground.

The idea of God

Hubbard recognizes the existence of a Supreme Being. His eighth dynamic is the urge towards survival as God or infinity. Although his followers have formed a Church, however, and though this Church has a creed and regularly publishes literature outlining its beliefs and practices, there is nothing in any of it that suggests that Hubbard's Supreme Being is a personal God, or that he is holy, or that he has revealed himself to humanity by becoming man, or that he loves man and in the person of his Son has provided the means of man's salvation. Scientologists *as Scientologists* do not see the need to worship God, have no sense of God's holiness and their own sinfulness, and appear to have no understanding of, or desire for, a personal relationship with God. If the words 'Life Force' were to be substituted for 'God' in their literature, we should seem to be nearer the truth. God, as understood by Christians, has no place in Scientology.

It is not surprising, therefore, that Scientology has no official doctrine of God. Each member is left to work out his own idea. There is no sense of God revealing himself in Christ and no place for authoritative scriptures. If a Scientologist has experienced a Christian upbringing, his ideas may still correspond roughly with the Christian view of the Trinity. If, on the other hand, he has been given a Jewish upbringing, he may continue to think of God as one Person. Again, if he joins the movement as an atheist, Scientology may take him to the point where he is prepared to recognize the existence of some kind of Life Force or Supreme Being. It will be left to the individual Scientologist to work out his own view. After all, what he finally decides about God will not affect his membership of the Church of Scientology one iota.

All of this is far removed from the Christian view of God derived from the Bible. Scripture opens with the words, 'In the beginning God', and the sixty-six books which follow concern themselves with the record of God in action. God reveals himself *to* man, *in* man and *for* man. The revelation reaches its climax in Christ, so that the writer to the Hebrews can say, 'When in former times God spoke to our forefathers, he spoke in fragmentary and varied fashion through the prophets. But in this the final age he has spoken to us in the Son whom he has made heir to the whole universe, and through whom he created all orders of existence.'[48]

Some Scientologists claim to be gnostics, those who *know*. It is important to remember, however, that we know what God is like only because he himself has taken the trouble

[48] Hebrews 1:1–2.

to show us. In our unaided search for God, our minds come up against a brick wall. We may be persuaded that behind order and design is a Divine Architect, that behind morality is a Moral Being, that behind creation is a Creator. Like Ron Hubbard we may happily speak of a Supreme Being. But of the nature of such a Being and of the way in which we may have fellowship with him, unaided human reason is able to tell us nothing. That is why we need Christ, and that is why we need the Bible.

What this means in practice is that our ideas of God must be checked against the view of God shown to us in Jesus Christ, the incarnate Word, and set out for us in the Bible, the written Word. Unless we are ready to do this, then (as with Scientology) any view of God will do. We may try to turn him into a cantankerous old man just waiting for us to step out of line, or, more probably, we may think of him as a benevolent Father Christmas who is not a bit concerned with the way we behave. If there is no objective revelation in Christ, then a Mary Baker Eddy, or a Charles Taze Russell, or a Joseph Smith, or even a Ron Hubbard, may be right. The Christian knows better, however, for his Lord and Master has said, 'Anyone who has seen me has seen the Father.'[49]

The place of Christ

Hubbard does mention Christ on one or two occasions, but only as one of the many sources of his views. Jesus of Nazareth is placed alongside the teachers of Hinduism, Buddhism, Taoism and Judaism, as providing part of the background of Scientology. The Church of Scientology does not proclaim that Jesus Christ is the Son of God who came to be the Saviour of the world. Rather, he is a great teacher who was feeling after the kind of wisdom contained more perfectly in the teachings of Scientology.

Not that Scientologists have any quarrel with Jesus Christ. One of their leaders told me, 'We are all-denomi-national . . . and of course we have no disagreement of Jesus Christ being the Son of God and the Saviour of

[49] John 14:9.

Mankind.' I felt it necessary to press him further, asking, 'Would it be fair comment to say that although Scientology has no disagreement with these doctrines, they are nevertheless not an essential part of Scientology's philosophy which is more akin to Buddhism?' He replied, 'Fair comment. Buddhism is right on the mark.'[50]

We shall not find in the sect's literature any statements denying Christ's deity, sonship, atonement and resurrection. Neither shall we find any affirming these doctrines. In fact, we shall have to look very hard to find any references to Christ at all. The Scientological error is not that it misrepresents Christ, but that *it does not represent him at all*. It is possible to find individual Scientologists who are prepared to say that Jesus is Saviour and Lord, but it seems fair to say that whatever faith in Christ exists in them is there not because of Scientology but in spite of it. In Hubbard's philosophy Christ is a non-starter. Scientology *is* Hubbard. Christianity *is* Christ. The two are not complementary but incompatible.

The way of salvation
One of the few dogmatic statements in Scientology's creed is the affirmation that man is basically good. The sect has no doctrine of sin. Men are either 'less able' or 'more able'. Whatever is wrong in a person is caused by engrams. Let that person submit himself to Scientology's processing, let him tell all to his auditor, let him make good use of his E-Meter as a twentieth-century confessional aid, and he will become a new man. This is Scientology's answer to the question, 'What must I do to be saved?'

I am not claiming for a moment that no-one is ever helped by Scientology's psychological techniques. Some lonely people find a tremendous 'release' in simply confiding in a good listener, and some may find this kind of help when talking to an auditor, though the dangers of unqualified people dabbling in psychological techniques cannot be disregarded.

Even the best forms of psychotherapy, however, cannot

[50] Personal correspondence with the author, 10 November 1969.

meet a person's basic spiritual need to establish a right relationship with God. In this respect, Scientology fails. Repudiating the clear teaching of the Bible that man is a sinner in need of a Saviour, Scientology tells man that he is basically good. Contradicting the scriptural view that man is unable to save himself, Scientology tells him that whatever is wrong in his personality can be put right by his own efforts. In support, Scientologists actually quote the Bible. 'For the fruit of the Spirit is in all goodness and righteousness and truth'[51] is said to mean that 'man is basically good'.[52] In this instance they fall victim to the kind of biblical interpretation favoured by sects such as Jehovah's Witnesses and Mormons. Taking the verse out of its context, they then impose their own peculiar interpretation upon it. There are several examples of this treatment of Scripture in *Scientology and the Bible*. On the whole, however, Scientologists are not guilty of this error, for they avoid it by ignoring the Bible altogether. Needless to say, in quoting Ephesians 5:9 in support of their doctrine of man's basic goodness, Scientologists do not refer to the rest of that epistle. Had they done so, they would have arrived at a very different conclusion. In chapter 2, for example, Paul writes, 'Time was when you were dead in your sins and wickedness.' Disclaiming any superiority over his Gentile readers in this respect, the apostle goes on, 'In our natural condition we, like the rest, lay under the dreadful judgment of God'. He then proceeds to show how God intervened to save man from his sin. 'But God, rich in mercy, for the great love he bore us, brought us to life with Christ even when we were dead in our sins; it is by his grace you are saved.'[53]

The position of the Bible

The sect's book, *Scientology and the Bible*, might lead the casual observer to believe that Scientology claims to derive its teaching from the Bible. A more careful study shows such a view to be mistaken. Occasionally Scientologists

---

[51] Ephesians 5:9, AV. [52] *Scientology and the Bible*, p. 48.
[53] Ephesians 2:1–5.

147

quote from the Bible, but Scientologists do not claim that the movement says the same things as the Bible about God, man and salvation. Indeed, in Scientology the Bible is conspicuous by its absence. Scientologists are prepared to recognize that the Bible is a holy book, one among many others, but they do not regard it as authoritative in matters of faith and conduct.

Consequently, the Bible is not read in Scientology services. As one of the sect's publications explains,

> We use the facts, the truths, the understandings that have been discovered in the science of Scientology. We do not read from the Bible (or the Koran, or the Torah, or the Vedic Hymns, for that matter) and say to the people assembled here – 'Now this is something you have got to believe.' There would be nothing wrong with quoting from the Bible or any other book as an illustration of man's continued *search* for truth to live by or as a contrast to some point that was being brought out in the sermon, but there is no necessity to quote from any other source in a Scientology Church Service.[54]

We may conclude therefore that Scientology believes:
1. that the 'facts', 'truths', or 'understandings' of Scientology are superior to anything taught in the Bible.
2. that the Bible has no authority in setting out what should be believed.
3. that the Bible is simply a story of man's search for truth.
4. that Scientology, unaided by the Bible, contains in itself all the 'revelation' man needs for salvation.

Christians will not need to be told that this view of the Bible is very different from that held by the Christian church. To us, the Bible is the written Word of God containing God's final revelation of himself in Christ, the incarnate Word of God. It is not merely the record of man's search for truth, but the record of Truth coming down to us in the person of God's Son. Although the Bible is not to be regarded simply as a handbook of doctrine, it neverthe-

---

[54] *Ceremonies of the Founding Church of Scientology*, p. 7.

less 'containeth all things necessary to salvation: so that whatsoever is not read therein, nor may be proved thereby, is not to be required of any man, that it should be believed as an article of the Faith, or be thought requisite or necessary to salvation'.[55]

God, Christ, salvation and the Bible. No-one could dispute that ideas about these four are crucial in Christianity. We have tried to see what Scientology says about them. It has been difficult, for Scientology says so little about them. To Scientology, these subjects are unimportant or, perhaps, optional extras. On this basis, therefore, it is fair to conclude that if Scientology is a religion at all it is a non-Christian religion. It is incompatible with the faith which says that God sent his Son to be the Saviour of the world.

Summary of main differences

Scientology	Christianity
Authority	
Although the Bible is used to bolster up the sect's ideas, the source of Scientology's philosophy and technology is Hubbard himself.	As the Word of God, the Bible is the yardstick against which all claims (including those of Hubbard) have to be measured.
God	
Although Hubbard and many of his followers are theists, belief in God is not essential to Scientology.	God is Trinity, Father, Son and Holy Spirit, three Persons within the unity of the Godhead.
Christ	
Christ has no essential or central place in the sect's teachings.	'God sent his Son to be the Saviour of the world.'

[55] Article VI of the XXXIX Articles of the Church of England.

Man is basically good, but 'engrams' (psychological hang-ups) prevent him from realizing his full potential. When released from these engrams through the sect's techniques, man begins to live on a higher level in terms of his own human achievement.

Man needs to be saved from sin and to be given new life. Both are available from God through faith in Christ.

9. The challenge of the sects

The main aim of this book has been to outline clearly and honestly the history, beliefs and practices of seven modern alternatives to Christianity. As a Christian I have not attempted to remain neutral, though I have done my best not to misrepresent the views of those with whom I must part company. Inevitably, however, some of the things I have written will have seemed negative. I make no apology for that, for sometimes it is necessary to be negative to achieve positive ends, as Paul showed in his letters to the Galatians and the Philippians. As promised in the Preface, however, it has always been my intention to end this book on a positive note. I must now try to make good that promise by indicating some of the ways in which the sects challenge us to look hard at our own beliefs and practices and then by suggesting what I believe we must do as we seek to share the good news of Jesus Christ with sect members.

In chapter 1 we considered seven characteristics which the sects have in common, and it was implied that in these areas mainstream Christianity has either a lesson to learn or a challenge to face. We now need to examine that implication in more detail.

Missionary zeal

The zeal with which the sects pursue their proselytizing activities must challenge us to ask questions about the earnestness of our own Christian witness. We have seen that sect members are ready to spend long hours in learning their beliefs and mastering their techniques and then in spreading their views to others. We may question their motives, pointing out that we as Christians receive salvation as God's gift and do not have to try to earn it by winning recruits. We may argue that sect members are indoctrinated and not encouraged to think for themselves, or that their so-called evangelistic activities have the dual purpose of repressing individuality and raising money. Be that as it may, there is no escaping from the fact that in many parts of the western world people are more likely to be confronted about religious matters by a sect member than by an orthodox Christian. This is a challenge we cannot ignore.

Unlike the sects, we do not claim to have a *new* message for the world, but we do claim to have *God's* message, the good news that God sent his Son to be the world's Saviour. Taking the Bible seriously, we know that this is the one message that everyone needs, that without it they are lost: for 'there is salvation in no one else, for there is no other name under heaven given among men by which we must be saved'.[1] Moreover, as Christians we have been given a clear command from Christ, 'Go therefore and make disciples',[2] 'You shall be my witnesses'.[3] Though we may deplore the methods the sects use, therefore, we have no excuse for lethargy or apathy in our own evangelistic outreach. Because we are Christians, we are committed to the task of making disciples.

Charismatic leadership

As we have seen, each of the sects started with its own special leader, who claimed a new revelation, a new interpretation, or a new technique. In practice, that leader then set himself up as another Christ, either by asking his followers to believe that he was another divine incarnation or by usurping the place of Christ in some other way. At this point, therefore, the challenge that comes to us from

[1] Acts 4:12, RSV.   [2] Matthew 28:19, RSV.   [3] Acts 1:8, RSV.

the sects is *not* that we, too, should look for a new charismatic leader, a kind of super-Christian to whom we can give blind devotion and absolute allegiance. Our truly charismatic leader is, and always has been, our Lord Jesus Christ. As Son of God, he alone has the right to make absolute demands, for all authority in heaven and on earth has been given to him.[4] He is the only one, therefore, to whom we, as Christians, can give that kind of complete devotion which the sect leader illegitimately demands of his followers, for we know that in his Person and through his work of redemption Christ has already achieved all that these others spuriously claim to offer.

Exclusive truth

Through their false prophets, spurious teachers and counterfeit messiahs the sects proclaim their heretical views as exclusive truths without which people cannot be saved. For reasons stated earlier, Christians reject these claims and at the same time maintain that they themselves have the truth, not so much in a body of doctrines, but rather in the Person of Jesus Christ who himself claimed to be *the* Truth.[5] Unlike members of the sects, Christians do not look for allegedly 'fuller' or 'newer' truths or enlightenments, no matter how or through whom they are claimed to have been mediated. They prefer the clear teaching of the New Testament that God, who previously spoke in many and various ways by the prophets, has now fully and finally spoken in his Son.[6] Because they are human, Christians do not claim to have fully grasped this truth, for there is so much more available to them in Christ than they have yet completely realized. Individually, they say with Paul, 'Not that I have already obtained this or am already perfect; but I press on to make it my own, because Christ Jesus has made me his own.'[7] Notwithstanding their own inadequacies in this respect, however, Christians are convinced that all truth is available in Christ, and not through any other source. They take to

---

[4] Matthew 28:18.   [5] John 14:6.
[6] Hebrews 1:1–2.   [7] Philippians 3:12, RSV.

heart the many warnings in the New Testament about false teachers and Antichrists and reject any suggestion of the need for secret and mysterious initiations. Whilst rejecting all such false claims, however, Christians need to face up to the challenge presented by the sects in fearlessly and unapologetically proclaiming what they believe to be true. Christ is the Truth. There is a body of Christian truth, a Christ-centred gospel, to be shared with the world. Unashamedly, we should say so.

Group superiority

The sects challenge us concerning the warmth of our Christian fellowship, for as noted earlier they emphasize the importance of the group and the strength which comes from belonging. The group becomes the welcoming community, the loving family of brothers and sisters, 'home'. Sect converts often point to this aspect of sect life as the one which attracted them most, and sometimes contrast it with the lack of fellowship they claim to have experienced within mainstream churches. Where this is true, it is a sad condemnation of our Christianity. We are the body of Christ, the family of God. Unlike the sects, we should not seek to claim superiority for the Christian community, for the church is the fellowship of forgiven sinners. But we should work to ensure that we are a welcoming community, where each member cares for the needs of others, where there is a mutual sharing of one another's burdens. It is this experience of belonging to a loving fellowship which is so sadly lacking in the world today and it should not surprise us if, failing to find this in a Christian group, some look elsewhere and are attracted to the sects.

This also raises another important issue, that of the kind of ministry we have within the Christian community. Most orthodox Christians today pay lip-service to the ideal of an all-member ministry within the church. In evangelical circles, especially, much is made of the 'priesthood of all believers'. More often than not, however, many Christian congregations still rely heavily upon the clergyman or minister to further the church's real work and tend to use lay people only in matters concerned with things like bricks and mortar and finance. In contrast, the sects take very seriously the full participation of every member in the life of the group. Each member is believed to have a significant part to play and, as a result, is made to feel important and wanted. There are no passengers.

Strict discipline

One of the characteristics of this modern age is the widespread rejection by western society of many of the moral values it inherited from Christianity. We speak about the permissive society and often, though often quite wrongly, assume that it is within this morally carefree and careless environment that young people feel completely at home. There is much evidence to the contrary, not least from the sects whose members clearly indicate that a significant number of people, most of whom are young, are ready to opt out of such a society in favour of one where a demanding code of conduct is rigorously applied.

I am not suggesting for one moment that the Christian churches should simply emulate the sects. Indeed, the kind of unthinking obedience often expected within such movements is far removed from that moral behaviour which springs from an obedient relationship with Christ motivated by love. What needs to be said, however, is that Christ does make demands, he does expect high standards, and that it is impossible to achieve either without discipline. For the Christian, however, it should never be an imposed discipline, but one which is the self-discipline of the Christian disciple who has taken to heart his Master's statement, 'If you love me you will obey my commands.'[8]

Repression of individuality

One of the most worrying aspects of much sect activity is the almost inevitable repression of individuality that takes place when a contact is drawn into the net of a sect's

[8] John 14:15.

proselytizing activities. I have written earlier of anxious parents who claim that their children have undergone a change of personality as a result of involvement in one of the sects. The reason is not hard to detect, for, as has been shown, it is a characteristic of many of the sects to submit new contacts to very long sessions of rigorous indoctrination. Those who respond in the manner the sect requires, surrender their individuality, cease to think for themselves, and swallow the sect's teaching hook, line and sinker.

Such methods raise several challenging issues for mainstream Christians. One of the most important – how to deal with those thus ensnared – will be considered in some detail at the end of this chapter. Another obvious challenge is the negative one of ensuring that in our own evangelistic activities we not adopt similar tactics. It is a noteworthy feature of the gospel records that Jesus always respected the freedom of the individual and never imposed himself or his teaching on those who wanted neither. We should do no less, even though at times it will mean that the individual will reject everything that we believe is for his eternal well-being. As Christians, we need constantly to remind ourselves that God made man free, free not only to respond to him and lovingly to serve him, but also to reject him and deliberately to disobey him. Of course God could have chosen to make us differently, so that we always obeyed him without question. Then when he pulled the strings, we would have performed the prescribed antics. In his wisdom, however, God chose to make us free; and if he respects the individual's freedom, we can do no less. Any attempt at manipulation or pressurized indoctrination can have no legitimate place in Christian evangelism. Proclamation there must be, but at the end of the day it is God who calls, Christ who saves and the Spirit who converts. We must never be tempted to play God.

Moreover, even when a person has responded to God's call, accepted the gift of salvation offered by Christ and been incorporated into Christ's body by the Spirit, his individuality must still be respected. God does not require us to remain 'babes' in Christ (as some of the sects would have us believe) but to continue to grow towards Christian maturity. Nor has he a uniform blueprint for all Christians, for he treats us as men and women made in his image, not as robots. He is the loving Father, and we are the sons and daughters to whom he has given responsibility. We must accept this fact, and so must the Christian community to which we belong.

Doctrinal deviations

As noted earlier, most of the challenges to mainstream Christian doctrine arising from the sects concern beliefs about authority, God, Christ and salvation. In the foregoing chapters, much has been written about the ways in which the sects deviate from the Christian church in these and other important areas. This book has not attempted in any way to provide a complete statement of orthodox Christian doctrine, so readers will need to look elsewhere if they wish to examine in detail what Christians believe. The main challenge of the sects at this point, however, is clear. Christians must be prepared to spend much more time studying their faith in order that they may 'contend for the faith which was once for all delivered to the saints'.[9]

Sharing the gospel with sect members

When all is said and done, however, there remains the one challenge that confronts any Christian in relation to those outside the Christian faith, that of knowing how best to share with them what he himself has found in Christ. Here, however, a word of caution is necessary. Established members of most of the sects examined in this book are past masters at proselytizing and at presenting their message so that it appears in the best possible light to those with whom they are discussing it. Sometimes they use deliberate deception, and often the most striking differences from Christianity are played down and the points of similarity are stressed. This means that some Christians, especially those young in the faith or without a sound grasp of Christian

[9] Jude 3, RSV.

teaching, will not always see through counterfeit claims and may be that more easily led astray. They are probably best advised to avoid contact altogether or, where this is impossible, to withdraw from it as soon as possible. Even a well-grounded and spiritually mature Christian will need to be on his guard and will wish to pray especially for the help of the Holy Spirit. Bearing all this in mind, however, a Christian will naturally be concerned about the spiritual needs of those ensnared by sects and will wish to do all he can to help them.

Love

As in all forms of evangelistic witness, love is of paramount importance, so we need to love sect members and pray for them. It is easy for us to regard them simply as enemies and to treat them accordingly. What we need to learn is that we must treat them as we would treat other non-Christians. They are our fellow men and women for whom Christ died.

Understanding

To love people involves trying to understand them, and part of that understanding will be trying to understand (though we cannot accept) what they believe. As we have seen, each of the seven sects in this book has its own elaborate doctrinal system or philosophical framework. Some of them use Christian terminology, others are more at home with Hindu words and ideas.

What needs to be noted, however, is that in practice most of them reject the major Christian doctrines concerning God, Christ and salvation, and have replaced the authority of the Bible with the alleged further revelations of a modern prophet, or have sought to control the teaching of the Bible by imposing upon it their own special interpretation, or look to other scriptures for their teaching, or, sometimes, have a combination of two or more of these attitudes.

The Bible

The question of authority is of course crucial, and the

Christian response to the members of any particular sect will need to vary in accordance with the stance which that sect takes on this vital issue. Where a sect claims a Bible-based authority (as in the case of the Armstrong movement and the Family of Love), Christians may feel that there is common ground between them and their contact.

Nevertheless, they will wish to discuss the unlikelihood of the position which the sect member will be trying to advance, that in, say, the middle of the twentieth century the leader of his sect has discovered the true interpretation of the Bible, and that for nearly 2,000 years before that, the Christian church has been completely mistaken in its views and living in sinful apostasy.

Where, however, a sect claims a superior revelation given by a modern prophet, there will be the need to discuss with the contact the kind of person that prophet has turned out to be and on what kind of evidence he bases his claims.

In the case of an appeal to other scriptures, Christians will wish to point out the kind of material these scriptures contain (such as those relating to Krishna and his sexual adventures), which bear very unfavourable comparison with the Bible narratives. Christians will wish to guard, however, against developing a hectoring style. As has often been said, it is possible to win an argument but lose the person concerned.

Respect

Christians should also be willing to learn from the sect member. In my experience, spanning more than twenty years studying the sects and contact with sect members, they are at least as sincere in their religious beliefs and practices as most Christians. They sincerely believe that they have found the truth by becoming members of their sect.

It is also worth remembering that many of them have turned to the sects after failing to find what they were searching for in orthodox Christian churches. Even though we shall have to disagree with their views, we must always respect them as persons and believe that they are sincere.

Finally, we should be ready at all times to offer them what we have in Christ. This means we must avoid the temptation to become involved in heated arguments (though disagreement will be inevitable). There may well be occasions when we shall want to discuss with them calmly and frankly details of belief and practice (always assuming that we have taken the trouble to discover where they stand). Against that background, we can then go on to tell them what we know of Christ and of what he has done for us. Having done that, we must trust God to bless our witness, for at the end of the day it is God who converts, not us.